CLEVERLY YOURS

HUMOROUS GLIMPSES OF LIFE AS A CHRISTIAN

BOB TERWILLIGER

Published 2020

Printed in the United States of America
ISBN 978-1951490591(p)
ISBN 978-1951490607 (e)

DartFrog Plus
4697 Main Street
Manchester, VT 05255
www.CanoeTreePress.com

Bible quotations are from The New International Version,
Copyright © 1978 by New York International Bible Society; and
from the Revised Standard Version, Copyright © 1946 and 1952 by
Division of Christian Education of the National Council Churches of
Christ in the United States of America.

*For Pat, who has always been there for me,
and whose love has been unfailing.*

CONTENTS

FOREWORD

During his fifteen years as Bethany Reformed Church's pastor, the Reverend Bob Terwilliger wrote approximately 150 front-page columns for the *Clarion*, Bethany's monthly newsletter. With July and August as vacation months, Pastor Bob wrote ten columns a year.

Wow! How does anyone come up with that many ideas? And they were clever ideas at that, with every column ending with some kind of "punnily yours" closing.

I was privileged to serve as co-editor with Lin O'Brien for twelve of those fifteen years, and we always looked forward to reading each column. We knew that however clever and entertaining the column, the best part was that it would always end with a spiritual and practical component that gave readers something to think over and apply to their own lives.

Editing Pastor Bob's column was fun and gave me great memories. I wish fun and good memories for you as you read – or re-read – some of Pastor Bob's favorite columns.

Janice Drolen
April 2020

INTRODUCTION

Church newsletters had their origin with the apostle Paul. In the first century, he was writing letters to various churches – Rome, Corinth, Ephesus, Thessalonica, Philippi, Colossae, and to an entire group of churches in the region of Galatia, cities which included Antioch, Iconium, Lystra, and Derbe.

Those letters contained everything from the deepest theological truths and instruction to personal greetings, from thanksgiving for gifts to explanations of Paul's current circumstances, and even included reprimands for the way some early Christians were behaving. The letters were circulated among the various churches and were probably read aloud at the gatherings of members. But they were treasured by the recipients and have become part of the official canon of the New Testament, speaking to their value for Christians and churches today.

But for 1900 years, those were the only letters to churches. Early in the 20th century, some churches began corresponding with the membership. An examination of the archives of the Reformed Church in America, the oldest Protestant denomination in the United States with a continuous ministry, revealed that the earliest known church newsletter was actually a form of newspaper, printed on newsprint, that contained the news of a group of Reformed Churches in Somerset County, New Jersey. According to Russ Gasero, the RCA Archivist, this newspaper contained basic information of activities in the roughly 20 churches that made up this group. It began running in 1903 and continued until 1931. Copies were distributed in each congregation.

Other churches began to produce newsletters in the mid- to late 50s, when church bulletins also began to make their appearance. This was a result of churches acquiring mimeograph machines, also known as stencil duplicators. These mimeo machines required a stencil to be prepared on a typewriter which was then loaded onto a rotating drum so that a pressure roller could force the ink through the stencil and onto the paper. By the early to mid-60s, church newsletters were regular productions of most churches. They provided a simple, inexpensive method of communicating with a church's membership.

Church newsletters typically had a message from the pastor and news about various church activities. Over the years they became much more elaborate productions and contained more information.

When I became the pastor of Bethany Reformed Church in Kalamazoo in 1998, the *Clarion*, our church newsletter was well established. It had been in existence since 1963 or thereabouts. It was expected that I would write the cover letter and oversee much of everything that would be included. The *Clarion* became a marvelous example of every-thing a church newsletter could be. Not only was I able to compose a cover letter, but there was a calendar of all the church events for the coming month, a listing of birthdays and anniversaries of church members and adherents, book reviews of new books added to the church library, news from the youth groups and the assistant pastors, music news, missionary letters, recipes from members, poetry, jokes, cartoons, financial reports, news from the consistory (the administrative leadership of the church), kids' pages with a variety of fun activities, lists of the shut-ins, prayer concerns, surveys, a column from the parish nurse, address changes, and other miscellaneous items. One popular item, developed by my wife, Patricia, was a column called "Getting to Know You." She interviewed each new member and discovered interesting facts and trivia about each one and made it into a matching quiz. In one column were the names of the new members; in the other column were the facts she discovered. She was good at getting people to reveal some of the most fascinating bits of information. This became so popular that she expanded it to include not only the new members, but the long-time membership of the church as well.

I decided that I would try to make my cover letter something unique that would entice people to read it. Another one-page devotional wouldn't cut it. So I took those common, everyday events that everyone could understand and relate to, and point out how our Christian faith is part of our daily lives. To add a little interest, I took liberties with what is known as the "complimentary close," the word ("Sincerely") or phrase ("Best wishes") that conventionally appears before the sender's signature. I tried to find a way to close each cover letter with a clever way to communicate what I was attempting to say. Hence, *Cleverly Yours*.

Because these cover letters were written over a period of 15 years, from 1998 to 2013, some of the content may be dated. Please forgive me. I made no effort to bring them up to date. The letters appear in no particular order, simply a random gathering of some of the more popular ones.

Thank you to Phil Stohrer, Joyce Santman, Sally Wells, Jeris Inglis, Mary Reeves, Lin O'Brien, and Jan Drolen for their editorial work on all these columns. I also need to thank all those members of the Bethany Reformed Church in Kalamazoo who continued to support and encourage me in writing these cover letters. Hopefully, each of you will also be able to find some humor and practical guidance in living out your faith in the 21st century.

To God be the glory.

Humbly yours,
Pastor Bob Terwilliger

AMAZING LOVE

I scrub toilets. Not just any toilets, mind you, just those at our house. In the rather unequal division of household duties that Pat and I have agreed upon, one of the chores I have done over the years is clean the bathrooms. I scrub toilets, tubs, sinks, mirrors - the whole works.

Pat appreciates it and I don't mind it all that much. There's a certain sense of accomplishment that comes from seeing the results of your efforts immediately.

A month or so ago, I was using a bathroom cleanser that contains bleach. (Believe me when I say that I'm very picky about what products I use.) I managed to get some on the sleeve of my shirt when I was leaning over the edge of the bathtub to apply some elbow grease. Sure enough, it bleached out my shirt, and one of my favorite ones, no less. But I refuse to throw the shirt away.

In fact, I continue to wear it, and if anyone were to ask about those white spots on my sleeve, I'd proudly proclaim the reason for them. I consider it almost a badge of honor. It shows that I clean bathrooms.

What shows up in your life that indicates who you are or what you do? Some people, like public safety officers, wear uniforms and badges that indicate their profession. Others, like doctors and nurses, carry stethoscopes that show some of what they do.

Jesus was able to display the scars on his hands and feet and in his side that prove he was the savior of the world who died on the cross for you and for me.

As Christians, we're supposed to display love for one another that all the world can see. (See John 13:34-35) Is your badge showing?

Vanish-ingly Yours,

Pastor Bob

WASHING MACHINES

A couple of weeks ago, our washing machine died. As typically happens, it was right in the middle of a load of laundry and the tub was full of dirty, soapy water. Pat had to dig the clothes out, wring them out as best she could, and go to a laundromat to dry those clothes and finish washing the rest of the laundry. When I got home, I scooped out all the water and finally sponged out the tub.

We had to buy a new washer. We checked out a variety of machines and checked the ratings in *Consumers Reports*. We ended up buying one that cost 5 times what I paid for my first car. And of course you have to buy new hoses as well. It's a wonder we didn't need a mortgage for a washing machine.

But I must say this new washer is something else. It's a high efficiency machine, which means you have to buy special detergent. But it only costs $36 a year in electricity. (Maybe that's only if you do 3 loads of wash annually.) I think you make up for the efficiency with the higher cost of detergent. It has a stainless steel tub, but NO agitator! It's strange to look inside and see this empty tub. It looks like something's missing. All washers used to have agitators, those things that stick up in the middle and go back and forth and up and down to get the clothes clean. But I do like the fact that the top is see-through so you can look in and watch what happens during the wash and rinse cycles.

It's an intelligent washer too. It automatically weighs the load of laundry and adjusts the amount of water it needs. It automatically balances itself if the load is too heavy on one side. That way, the washer doesn't vibrate so much that it walks across your basement floor.

The most amazing thing, though, is that in the spin cycle, when the water is being spun out of the wet clothes, it rotates at over 1000 revolutions per minute. That's almost 17 revolutions per second! When Pat put in the first load of laundry, I stood there and watched what happened. That spin cycle blew me away. Pat says I must not get out much if I get my thrills by standing in the basement and watching clothes being washed for the entire 51 minute cycle. I must say, it was more exciting than much of what's on TV.

It occurs to me that we have a spiritual washing machine as well. The Holy Spirit works to agitate our consciences to make us aware of our sinfulness and our need for cleansing. Then Jesus, in an ultra-high efficiency manner, washes out the stains of sin through his shed blood and broken body. Our souls have never been so clean.

Tide-fully yours,

Pastor Bob

UNDER CONSTRUCTION

On a recent trip to New York, I counted (no comments, please, about my OCD) no less than 31 construction zones. Some were only half a mile long or so; some were much longer – as long as 12 miles in one case. In most cases the traffic had to go from two lanes to one lane, but at other times, it was from three lanes to two. But whichever it was, it always caused traffic to slow down and back up. And wouldn't you know it, this was right after I preached a sermon on patience and confessed my own frustration and lack of patience on the highways.

God has a way of getting us the message. Plus, the speed limit in a construction zone is only 45 or 50 mph, with large warning signs telling drivers that fines are doubled in construction zones. Michigan warnings are much more intimidating: Kill a worker, go to jail!

In some cases entire lanes were being repaved. In others, it was shoulder work. And in a few, it was repairs to a bridge over the highway. For the record, 24 of the construction zones were in Pennsylvania, but Ohio had the longest ones. In Michigan, there was only one – near an exit on I-69, just north of Coldwater.

I'm wondering if this says anything about the amount of money the various states have available to repair our infrastructure or is simply an indication of the priority given to such projects.

I think if you total all the workers I saw in all 31 construction zones, there were 4 actual workers, with about 157 observers and supervisors. I think all make about $35 or $40 an hour. Not bad for leaning on a shovel. But it WAS hot, so maybe they get extra credit for being out there under the sun.

At any rate, driving slowly as I was through those construction zones gave me time to think that we as Christians are always in a construction zone. God is always working on our lives, upgrading, making improvements, sometimes slowing us down to make the necessary repairs.

There used to be lapel buttons that some church members had that read like this: PBPGINFWMY. When people asked what it meant, it was: Please Be

Patient. God Is Not Finished With Me Yet. And that's the way it is. We're always under construction.

Driving slowly,

Pastor Bob

BEAUTIFUL FEET

My wife has pretty feet. Or at least she used to. First of all, they're dainty - small, actually. She only wears a size 6 shoe, or sometimes a 6 1/2. Her toes angle very nicely from the big toe to the pinky toe. If you took a ruler and put it on top of her big toe and touched it to the top of her little toe, it would touch every other toe along the way.

My feet are not shaped like that. First of all, I have a high arch. Secondly, my toes are similar to my fingers. In other words, my second and third toes are both longer than my big toe, just as my index finger and middle finger are both longer than my thumb.

I always thought that was normal - until I saw Pat's toes. Now hers look normal and mine look deformed. In addition, a couple of my toes have been broken through the years and are now shaped like bent macaroni.

But I said her feet used to be pretty. Now there's a strange lump on one side of the ball of her left foot. It's not ugly or anything. It just ruins the symmetry from before. But it's not just what her feet look like. She can do strange things with them. She can spread all her toes apart like you can do with your fingers. When she does that, not one toe touches another toe. Splayed toes do not look normal. It looks like she's getting ready to palm a basketball with them.

There's no way I can do that. I think a couple of my toes have been Super-Glued together. I can separate them with my fingers, but not just by using my individual toe muscles the way Pat can do it. With her toes spread out like that, the width of her foot goes from something like 4 inches to 4 1/2 feet. And they said Bigfoot was a myth! And how she gets those feet into some of her pointy-toed shoes, I'll never know.

You should really examine your own feet sometime. They may be pretty or dainty or ugly, old, and deformed. Your toes may be crooked or straight. You might have a high arch or flat feet. Your toenails might look nicely polished and pedicured, or they may be ingrown, yellow, and thick, and in need of a highly skilled neurosurgeon to trim them. Feet are really funny things when you stop and look at them.

But feet are also Biblical. The Psalmist writes about them: "The Lord set my feet on a rock and gave me a firm place to stand." (40:2) "He has kept my feet from stumbling." (56:13) "Your word is a lamp to my feet." (119:105) Jesus washed the feet of his disciples and tells us we should do the same for one another. And Paul, in his letter to the Romans, quotes the prophet Isaiah when he says: "How beautiful are the feet of those who bring good news!" (Romans 10:15) So you see, no matter how mangled, misshapen, or twisted your feet may seem, they really are beautiful - at least in the eyes of the Lord.

Podiatrically yours,

Pastor Bob

BE A LIVING TREE

'Tis the season! We tramp into the woods, or to the local mall, and find the perfect tree. We cut it down, or select it carefully, then bring it home and try to make it look as nice in the house as it did outdoors. Surely we can hide that gaping hole. Turn it this way a little more; no that way. There, that's good enough. By the time all the decorations are on it, no one will notice. Why is the trunk on these trees never straight?

Or maybe you've moved beyond the real tree phase and have gone to an artificial tree. Perfectly shaped, no needles to drop, no need to water it, no smell – maybe the lights are already on it, or built into it. Pat and I used to have an artificial tree, but it died.

The concept of using an evergreen for a Christmas tree has to do with the symbolism of everlasting life. Even though the other trees lose their leaves and go into a dormant stage, the evergreen doesn't.

It represents the eternal life that is ours because of the coming of the Christ child into our world.

So what have we lost when we use an artificial tree or one that has been cut down? There's no life in either one. They're both dead. I'm not arguing for using live trees, although some folks do that. They come with a root ball, covered with dirt, and wrapped in burlap so the tree can be planted outdoors in the spring. But I think we need to remember that the tree isn't just another pretty holiday decoration. The Psalmist says that the people of God are "like trees planted by streams of living water, which yield their fruit in its season, and their leaves do not wither. In all they do, they prosper." (Psalm 1:3) In other words, YOU'RE a Christmas tree! You have everlasting life. Jesus, who is the living water, nourishes us and refreshes us and sustains us daily. Maybe we should hang Christmas balls from our ears and drape ourselves in tinsel and garland to remind ourselves of this.

May all the joy and peace of Christ be yours in this holy season.

Coniferously yours,

Pastor Bob

FIT IN BODY AND SOUL

I really don't like to exercise. But I know I need to exercise, especially in the winter months. In the spring and summer I get lots of exercise. I play golf, I walk, I ride a bike, I mow my lawn, I swim. When the weather is nice, it's easy to be outside and take advantage of those sunny days to stay active.

But in the winter, say from late October until about the first of April, it's all too easy to curl up in an easy chair with a good book and just veg out. When I lived in Illinois, I used to play racquetball a couple times a week with some pastor friends, and that was great. Now I have become what they call a "sedentary American."

This winter, I decided to do something different. The community education program offers a 12-week class of exercise called Basic Training. It meets every Monday, Wednesday, and Friday at the

SWAT Fitness Club from 12:00 to 12:45. I signed up. I figured it would be good to get out of the office at lunch time and get some physical activity.

I assumed that because it was called BASIC Training, it was intended for those who were just getting started with exercise. You know – it's BASIC.

WRONG! Well, maybe it's good to get out of the office, and I know it's important for me to get some exercise, but I think this class will kill me.

It's not BASIC, like in your A-B-Cs. It's BASIC like Basic Training for the Marine Corps! In just the first couple of weeks, we have done aerobics, flexibility work, weight training, Taebo (that boxing style of exercise where you punch the air a lot), circuit training, and enough other stuff to make me sore all over. I suppose it'll do me some good – if I survive it.

Pat tells me it'll get easier, and I need to be committed to this. That's easy for her to say. I'm the one with the sore back, arms, legs, stomach, and everything else that's still part of my body.

This got me thinking about our spiritual discipline. Many times we determine at the beginning of the year to pray more, read the Bible more, and in general, be a nicer person. Our intentions are wonderful. But as with physical exercise, it requires a real commitment, and that's not always easy.

But God promises us that if we are faithful, it'll get easier with time and be good for our overall spiritual health and well-being. Plus, prayer and Bible reading won't kill you.

Sorely yours,

Pastor Bob

YIELD TO GOD'S SIGNS

A couple of weeks ago I was driving home from the grocery store when my car went through a malevolent transformation. Everything was fine one moment, and the next, there was a thunderous roar that seemed to emanate from the very bowels of the earth. I couldn't hear myself think. The car was vibrating from the sound alone. People in other cars were staring. The faster I tried to go to get away from the sound and back home, the worse it got. I finally made it to a muffler shop, coasting when I could, where they showed me that the resonator pipe had broken into two sections. "Ah, of course," I said, not having the slightest clue what a resonator pipe was. Half an hour later, and a hundred bucks poorer, I was on the road again with a softly purring vehicle.

There's an important lesson here, I think. I shouldn't have ignored that gentle growl I'd heard for a week or so. I figured I had a small hole in my muffler. After all, my car had 128,000 miles on it, and still had the original exhaust system. But a car can go a long time with a little hole in the muffler before it needs replacing, right? Wrong! That little rumble was a warning that I needed to take care of something and not put it off.

God gives us warning signals in our lives as well. We would do well to heed them, whether they be the gentle growls of a friend, the kindly words of Scripture, or the whispers of a guilty conscience – before they become the deafening roar of a life gone bad. It's easier to fix something before it gets out of hand, and a lot less embarrassing. Sin can start as just a tiny pinhole in one aspect of life, but left alone, and untended, it can shatter entire lives. Listen to the warnings God sends your way. And get them fixed before the pipes fall off in your life.

Quietly yours,

Pastor Bob

MIRACLES HAPPEN!

It wasn't the best shot I ever hit. It certainly wasn't pretty. But the result was exactly what we always hope for and seek to attain – a hole-in-one!

I'll be the first to tell you it was lucky. I've since read that the odds are something like 1 in 8,000 for making a hole-in-one. Obviously, the pros do it more often; the rest of us, less so. But when it does happen, we are overjoyed, thrilled, struck speechless.

Fortunately there were witnesses – and from our church golf league, no less. They say God punishes pastors who golf on Sunday by allowing them to get a hole-in-one. How is that punishment? Who can they tell that they were playing golf on a Sunday?

Sometimes the same thing happens in life as happened to me on the golf course. Even though we may not give it our best shot, even though we think we weren't very successful, God rewards our perseverance with positive results.

We may think our witness wasn't fruitful, or our words less than helpful, or maybe the example we set wasn't all that great. But then we hear that somehow our words or our actions really made a difference in someone else's life. That's the miracle of God's Spirit at work in us and through us, and in spite of us.

A hole-in-one may or may not be a miracle, depending on your point of view. For me, it almost certainly was. But then, God provides miracles every day of our lives.

Miraculously, and Nicklausly yours,

Pastor Bob

THE TARDY NEWSPAPER

Well, the newspaper was late again on Saturday. I had to call the Gazette office and they eventually delivered the paper around 10:30 a.m.

I hate it when the paper is late on Saturday. It's the only morning I have time to sit with a cup of coffee and spend time with the newspaper. It's one of my life's little pleasures.

The Gazette is only a morning paper on Saturday and Sunday, and obviously, I don't take time on Sunday mornings to read the paper. I may glance at the obituaries before I head to church, but that's about it.

We had a great delivery person for a while. He was courteous, hard working, and anxious to please. I tipped him pretty well for his effort. But now we have a new delivery person, and the results are less than desirable. I hate it when the paper is late.

I know delivery persons try hard to do a good job, but sometimes the car won't start, sometimes the paper itself is late getting to the delivery person, and sometimes there's illness in the family, or a good excuse why the paper is late. But I don't know the reason. All I see is the timeliness of the delivery, the final result. It's either there on time, or it's late. I hate when it's late.

I think God must get frustrated with us at times. Sometimes the results of our efforts are less than they should be. We're often late in fulfilling our promises to God.

We make solemn vows to act like Jesus, to share the good news of the gospel, to extend the cup of cold water to the thirsty and food to the hungry, to visit the sick, to befriend the lonely. But then something else comes up. Often it's a good excuse, or so we think.

Sometimes God must sit back on a Saturday morning or a Tuesday afternoon or a Wednesday evening and think, "Well, I'll just sit here and relax and watch my child fulfill his promise. What a pleasure it will be." But then we disappoint him once more. Fortunately, God knows our heart, is willing to forgive, and has an eternity to wait for us to follow through. But he must really hate it when we're late.

Often tardy, but always forgiven,

Pastor Bob

THE CHOICE IS YOURS

A couple weeks ago I was in the store buying some toothpaste. I was blown away by the selections. Normally, Pat buys the toothpaste and I just use it. But it was my turn to buy it. There in the toothpaste aisle I stood aghast as I gazed upon the variety and number of options available. You've got all your different brands: Colgate, Crest, Aquafresh, etc. Then there are the different size tubes – 2 ounces, 4 ounces, 8 ounces, etc. And there are the various choices within each brand and size. Whitening, tartar fighting, extra-whitening, for sensitive teeth, extra-extra-whitening, mint-flavored, cinnamon-flavored, bubble gum-flavored (for kids I assume), and the list goes on. You don't even have to buy a tube of toothpaste. You can buy it in a pump container. I counted them all. Considering all the different sizes, different brands, different flavors, different emphases, you have your choice, in that store anyway, of 159 toothpastes, 48 variations of Crest alone.

This got me thinking about when I worked at the Kellogg Company. There we believed in brand proliferation also. The more varieties, the more flavors, the more sizes, the more of anything you put out there, the better your chances of making a sale. You've got more shelf space and more options to lure the customer to your product.

So I went over to the cereal aisle, expecting it to be similar to the toothpaste section. Man, was I ever wrong! Standing there for about a half hour, making a fool of myself, I counted what I saw in the cereal section. I think I have this accurate because I took notes while I was doing this. Counting brands, flavors, sizes, etc., there were 372 choices of cereal, 59 of them just hot cereals.

You can buy cereal with black currants and walnuts, or with strawberries, blueberries, yogurt, cinnamon, apples, bananas, maple, chocolate, flax seed, almonds, pecans, vanilla, peanut butter, raisins, dates, cranberries, high fiber, 100% of your daily recommended vitamins, extra calcium, or any combination of those. There are cereals for active people (Seitenbacher), weight-loss cereals (Special

K), old-fashioned cereals (Kix Shredded Wheat), patriotic cereals (Uncle Sam's) kid cereals (Dinosaur Eggs, Fruity Pebbles, Cap'n Crunch, Sponge Bob, and Bunny-Os). You can buy cereal with names like Cocoa Beach or Mountain Medley, or Muesli or Kashi. There are natural cereals, organic cereals, and highly-processed sugar-laced cereals. You can even buy cereals with, ahem, somewhat medicinal properties: All-Bran, Bran Buds, etc.

Fortunately, the Bible tells us this about our faith: Hear, O Israel, (and everybody else!) the Lord our God, the Lord is One. (Deut. 6:4) There's no possibility of making the wrong choice.

Yours, without having to choose,

Pastor Bob

GET IT CLEAN

I discovered something amazing last week. The car I drive, a 2000 Toyota Camry, is green. For months I thought I was driving a white car, but then I went through a car wash, and what do you know? It's green! I wash my car once every three years, whether it needs it or not. I'm told that some folks wash their cars every week. Why? It just gets dirty again.

After our long winter, the car accumulated a great deal of road grime and salt, so I thought I should probably go ahead and wash it. But as I pulled out of the car wash, it began to rain. My son Rob tells me that in the Detroit area, some car washes will allow you to get the car washed again for free if it rains within 24 hours of the first wash. They could go broke around here.

There are lots of choices for car washes. You can do it by hand, with a bucket of soapy water and a sponge and chamois, or you can go to a self-service wash where you put several quarters in the slot and get a good 15 to 20 seconds of spray before you have to feed the machine again. Either way, you end up soaking yourself.

For a few dollars though, you can go to one of the automatic car washes where your car is towed along on a conveyor belt while the sprays do their thing. You have several choices: the regular wash, the classic wash, or the ultimate wash. I'm not sure how much difference there is, but with the more expensive washes you get things like undercarriage sprays, wheel washes, a coat of wax, anti-streaking goo, and rain repellent. With the ultimate wash, you also get a hard spray that's guaranteed to remove tar, bird droppings, loose molding, radio antennas, and side mirrors.

Things are different when it comes to our souls. They get dirty every day. A dirty car will continue to run, but dirty souls can shut us down for eternity. Sin stains our souls and makes us unworthy. They need washing on a regular and on-going basis, but there's no self-service soul wash. The good news is we don't need to go to some gas station or car wash facility to get our souls clean. We can go right to the manufacturer who will do it for free. God assures us that if we confess our sin, he is faithful and just, and will forgive our sin, and cleanse us from all unrighteousness. (1 John 1:9) This is the good news of Easter, that Jesus died and rose again to forgive our sins and clean our souls. Isaiah reminds us: "though your sins are like scarlet (grimy and salt-stained), they shall be white as snow."

Yours with a dirty car, but a clean soul,

Pastor Bob

DINING WELL

We had a wonderful time at our Christmas dinner, didn't we? Being at the Kalamazoo Country Club was a real treat for all of us. The food was great, the entertainment was enjoyable, and the service was out of this world. Thanks to everyone who made this occasion such a fabulous time in this holy season. But eating at the country club got me thinking about other such feasts.

Have you ever sat down to a fancy dinner, either in a high-end restaurant or maybe at a friend's house, only to notice that there are some 46 pieces of silverware? There are about 13 different forks, 4 or 5 knives, and about 73 different spoons, all different sizes and shapes. And they're located all over the place. Some are at the left side of your plate, some are at the right, some are above the dinner plate, and the rest take up space wherever there's room. There are salad forks and dinner forks and dessert forks. You have your choice between soup spoons, coffee spoons, teaspoons, tablespoons, dessert spoons, and some other spoons for which no one has ever discovered a purpose.

In addition to all the silverware, you'll often see different plates of various sizes as well. One is typically a dinner plate, one is for salad, another is for your bread, and there may be one there for dessert. But sometimes, at a restaurant, they'll take away what you thought was the dinner plate when they take your salad plate, leaving you wondering if you're going to have to eat the entrée off the tablecloth.

And the glassware can be confusing as well. In some cases, there are goblets for water, and different sizes and shapes of wine glasses for the different kinds of wine. When you don't order wine in the restaurant, they take away those glasses at least. And there's usually a coffee cup there, sitting on a saucer. And how do you know which glass is yours? Do you reach to the left or to the right? I often end up drinking my wife's water because I went right instead of left, or left instead of right. Oh well...

All these pieces of silverware and dinnerware and glassware leave hardly any room for the actual food you are there to consume. And there's certainly no room for your elbows on the table, as if any of us would be boorish enough to do such a thing. But eventually the food comes, and we dine well, leaving the table satisfied and happy.

There's another feast we can all look forward to. It's the feast at the great banquet table in God's heaven, where, as John tells us in Revelation, there will never be hunger or thirst. I'm sure there will be plenty of food, lots of laughter, and all of eternity to enjoy it and figure out which fork to use.

Well fed and happy,

Pastor Bob

TRASH OR TREASURE

A box full or hangers, another box full of paper bags, and yet another box filled with pieces of Styrofoam. These were some of the items I found recently when I was in New York to clean out my parents' home. I can hear my Dad now: "You never know when you might need a piece of Styrofoam about four inches long and an inch thick."

My parents both grew up during the Depression and, as a result, tended to save everything: boxes filled with rubber bands, balls of string, old clothes that needed to be patched, pieces of cloth to be used as patches, used pieces of aluminum foil. You name it, they probably had it. My mother used to sew some of her own clothes, and I found boxes of old patterns from the '50s, and other boxes filled with pieces of material that were already cut out and still had the pattern pinned to them. Just needed to be sewn together.

I came across some of the toys and games that my brothers and I used to play with as kids: Mousetrap, Operation, Put-n-Take, Skunk, Life, Careers, Pick-up-Sticks. There was an old train set, hula hoops, and a pogo stick. I found my ice skates from when I was about 12, and a cracked hockey stick. My mother saved clothes from when we were kids, all carefully folded and packed away in plastic bags. There were probably 200 empty margarine tubs with lids, and old jelly jars that we used as drinking glasses. Trash or treasure?

I also came across several items with emotional impact: letters my dad sent to my mom when he was overseas in World War II, calendars and expense books my dad kept from when he was in college, letters I sent to my folks when I was in college, autograph books from when my folks were in high school. Reading through them brought back bittersweet memories, and not a few tears. It made me pause when deciding what to do with all this "stuff" that had gathered dust in my parents' home for years. Obviously many of these things meant a great deal to my folks or they wouldn't have saved them. And while they had some meaning for me as I read through them, what could I do with them? Trash or treasure?

Ultimately, just about everything went in the

dumpster. It seemed a shame to discard things that were so important to my parents, yet what was the alternative? It didn't make sense for me to save all this. I would have simply been more "stuff" in our house. I did save the baseball glove my dad used in high school, and the letters from the war. There were some old pictures I brought home as well.

Most of our lives, and our homes, are filled with just such combinations of trash and treasure. And ultimately, all will have to be sorted and either saved or discarded. But Jesus reminds us that our true treasure is in heaven, that we shouldn't be quite so concerned with the transitory things of this earth. "Do not store up for yourselves treasures on earth, where moth and rust consume...but store up for yourselves treasures in heaven...For where your treasure is, there your heart will be also."

Fortunately, I know both my mom and dad are now in heaven, enjoying the treasures they've stored up there. But I was the one who had to deal with all the trash.

From the basement, amid the dust,

Pastor Bob

SURVIVAL

A group of us were talking the other night and came to the conclusion that it's a wonder any of us survived our childhood. Cars didn't have seat belts. We didn't get buckled into infant seats in our parents' cars. In fact, many of us rode down the highway lying flat in the back of the station wagon or hatchback, or maybe even tucked onto the shelf in the back window.

We never wore helmets when we rode our bikes. We didn't have knee pads when we roller skated down the middle of the street. We probably chewed on windowsills covered with lead-based paint. And maybe we even ran with scissors without putting our eyes out. We snacked on Twinkies, Ho-Hos, and Ding Dongs instead of baby carrots and low-fat yogurt. My brothers and I even had a little vial of mercury out of an old thermometer and we'd play with it. Put it in your hand and watch how it would form little globules, then coalesce and go back together. Fun stuff, that mercury, all silvery and cool to the touch. Who knew it was poisonous? We didn't worry about pollution or global warming or toxins in the water. We probably swam in lakes filled with e-coli bacteria. We climbed on monkey bars that did not have soft landing areas. Terrorism was not part of our vocabulary. IEDs were unknown.

We did, however, live through the Cold War and the Cuban Missile Crisis, and the threat of nuclear holocaust. Many of us as children learned to go into the hallways at school, sit facing the wall, and put our hands behind our necks, which was supposed to protect us in the event of a nuclear bomb going off. There was no concern over tick-borne illnesses. One of the biggest worries was polio, a crippling disease, but Dr. Salk took care of that with his miracle vaccine. Cigarettes were even advertised by doctors as being good for you!

Were those days really so care-free? Or were we and our parents simply oblivious, unaware of the dangers of living in our world? Certainly the Bible reminded us of sin and its consequences. It told of the temptations we would face and the trials and tribulations of life. But most importantly, God pro-tected us. David reminds us that "The Lord...will not forsake his faithful ones. They will be protected forever." (Psalm 37:28)

Still surviving, still protected,

Pastor Bob

LOVE LIKE THIS

Pat and I have a religious dog. He's a golden retriever named Aslan. We got him from the humane society when we lived in Illinois and our son, Jim, named him after the golden lion in the *Chronicles of Narnia*. (The Lion is the Christ figure in C.S. Lewis' books that include *The Lion, the Witch, and the Wardrobe*, but that's another story.) So our dog has a religious name to start with. Secondly, he prays. Not really, I guess, but we taught him to "say his prayers." He sits on his haunches, puts both paws on a chair, then puts his head down on his paws. He looks like he's praying. He'll stay like that until we say "Amen." Then he gets his treat. Maybe there are some folks in church we could teach that trick to. Just kidding!

The real reason I say he's religious is because he practices what Jesus told us to do. Jesus said we should love one another the way he loves us, with an unconditional love. And that's exactly what Aslan does. We call him a "smooch pooch" because all he wants to do is love and be loved. It doesn't matter if you're gone for 5 days or 5 minutes, when you return to the house, the dog greets you as if you'd been gone for 5 years. If you scold him, he slinks off and hides for a minute or two, then comes begging for forgiveness and more love. Those of you who have dogs know what I'm talking about.

It's wonderful to be loved with that kind of love. No strings attached. And that's how God loves us. Sometimes it's easier to feel a dog's love than God's love, but his love is greater than that of any animal. I have at times wondered if God didn't give us dogs to teach us about the nature of his love. In fact, dog spelled backward is "God!" Think about that for a while.

Doggedly yours,

Pastor Bob

PLEEZ FIXX TH RUUF

As I rite this thare is a tremendous cacophony of noize that impedes my abilty to concentrat, so if there are errors of speling ore Grammer or if there seems to be words msssing it's becuz of ths horribul NOIZE! It seemes that our flat roof, the Ruuf over the offisses an the Centnnnl Rom hav a problem with leeks. No not onions, I mean leaks - the watr kind. The roooofers are here to fix it. This is not the furst time eether. So while there up their pounding and scraping and tarring and poundingand stomping, I'm down here trying to get something written for the Calrion.

Why ennyone builds flat roofs in Michagin is sumthin i will never unnerstan. It probly haas somethin to do with cost, but in this climate, with snow, rain, ice, did I mention rain? It doesn't seem to make cents, although maybe it saves dollars. Tha's a joke.

This repair business izzn't cheep either. This time it's ONLY (Ha! Ha!) a thousand bucks. It's been more before, and the estimate to do it rite is about 8thousand $. But when you hav a building tha'ts beeen here for this menny yeers, ther are bound to be nessessary repares. but in the meantime, its hard too get enny work dun. Or atleast too get it done wel. Pleeze bare with mee.

The allternativ is to let things go, but thenn weed have a flud in the offissses. Alrady thare are sealing tiles that are bulging with the water that has come thru our leeky ruuf. Just what we neeed is for thoze tiles to come krashing down wit a deluge that wud rival what Noah had to endoor.

I gess we have to tolerate such inconveeenienses in order to keeepe our building safe and able to last antoher hunderd yeers or so. But it shur makes is hardd for me to konsentrate.

I'm shur you''ve all had to make repares on your homes as well. It's not always plesent to hav workers in yur house or to put up wit the messs thay sometimes mak. God also makes repares in our lives, and that ken be messsy too. He may hav to doo some scraping and chipping ore some pounding and polishing. But ultimately it''s for the bes.. 'wE NEEd thoze fixes. WE neDD God to wurk on us.. WeE hav to be impruved and only God can ddo it. So we aks God to fix us, to forgiv us, too change us. And wee thankkkk him wen all th wurk is dun.

Yurs unner repare......!,

Pester Bub

A NEW GIZMO

I have a new gizmo, although Pat calls it my new obsession. For my birthday, I got an e-reader. For those of you who've been oblivious to the commercials this year, an e-reader is an electronic device on which you can download books - lots of books. There are several brands, of which the Amazon Kindle is probably the most popular, although I've been hearing and seeing a lot of ads for the Barnes and Noble Nook.

I didn't buy either one of those. I bought a Sony. I did a lot of research before committing to the Sony. The Kindle requires you to buy books from <u>amazon.com</u>. The Nook allows you to read any book in the Barnes and Noble store for one hour. The Sony has access to Google Books, which has over 2 million books available, some free and some for sale. But the real clincher for me was that the Sony allows me to download e-books from the public library system. Any books in the public domain, which includes most of the classics, are free from Google, and most contemporary books are available from the library. And the whole thing is wireless! No connections to anything. You don't even have to go to the library.

This device has enough internal memory to store about 3500 complete books. But it also has external storage capacity, which means you can insert a memory card to store an entire library, no matter how many books you've got. It also plays MP3 files, which is music, so you can put on your earphones and listen to music while you read. You can even subscribe to magazines or newspapers and they will come automatically to your e-reader.

To use it, you call up a book and each page is shown on the screen, which is especially designed so you can even read it in full sunlight, which you can't do with a normal computer. To turn the page, you just push a button, or, because the Sony has a touch screen, you just swipe your finger across the screen, like you might do with a real book.

It has 12 built-in dictionaries, including foreign language dictionaries, which means if you come across a word you don't know, you just tap that word twice and the definition comes up on the screen. You can use a stylus, or your fingernails to make notes in the margins, or to just doodle if you want. It's only one-third of an inch thick, and about the size of a small paperback. I find the whole contraption nothing short of amazing! You can see why Pat calls it my new obsession. I've read 4 books on it in the 5 weeks since my birthday.

Now granted, there are some drawbacks. You don't have the feel and heft of a real book. There's no smell like you sometimes get with a book, especially a new one. And you can't fill your bookshelves with an impressive stack of real books. But you don't have to worry about overdue fines, because an e-book from the library automatically disappears when the due date arrives.

I love books. Always have, always will. And I'll still go to the library to check out the real thing, and I'll still go to Barnes and Noble. But now, when we go to the beach, I can just take along my e-reader instead of a whole bag of books.

Occasionally you'll come across someone's estimate of the 100 greatest books of all time. I have my own list, but there are only 66 on my list. They're the 66 books of the Bible. And I figure if God came up with 66 books, I'll just have to make sure I read all of them and read them carefully, whether they're on my e-reader or in hard copy. Those are the books that really matter. They contain the Word of Life.

Don't bother me, I'm reading,

Pastor Bob

HOW ALARMING!

Bethany has an alarm system. That may seem odd to some of you, and maybe it's a sign of the times that a church has to have an alarm. But unfortunately, it's necessary. There are little magnetic sensors on doors and motion detectors in various locations throughout the building.

When you first come into the church, you have 60 seconds to enter the appropriate code into the little keypad. If you don't enter it correctly (you get 3 tries), or don't do it soon enough, sirens go off and a silent alarm is sent to the security company which then notifies the police.

When the police are notified, they send an officer or two to our location to see if there is indeed an illegal entry or if it's a false alarm. This happens several times every year because someone opened the wrong door first or forgot the correct code to enter or because we did indeed have someone in the church.

Once it even happened because the alarm was set while folks were still washing dishes after coffee time and when they went to leave, they set off the alarm.

Our phone rang last Tuesday night (Wednesday morning actually) at 1:30 a.m. It was the security company that monitors the alarm. Something triggered the system and they were sending the police to investigate. I was called to get out of my nice warm bed, get dressed, and meet the police at the church for an inspection.

The officer and I walked around the outside of the building and couldn't find any footprints in the snow leading to or from the church. Then we went inside. I shut off the alarm and we proceeded to do a walk-through of the entire building, opening doors, checking closets, and going into every nook and cranny where someone might be hiding. All the doors were locked, all the windows were secured, and there was no evidence that anyone had been inside. Nothing had been tampered with. It looked like a false alarm.

We have several zones that indicate where the alarm was triggered. We can even track an intruder's path inside. But there was nothing. A subsequent inspection of the system showed that everything was working properly. What could it have been?

We'll never know, I guess. It's just one of those mysteries that often accompany modern technology.

It just seems a shame that we have to have burglar alarms in a church. It used to be that church doors were always left unlocked for any poor soul that wanted to enter for a few moments of prayer or silent sanctuary. People never stole anything from a church for fear that a lightning bolt from heaven would strike them dead on the spot. There are never more than a few dollars on the premises because the offerings are deposited on Sunday morning right after church. But there are some computers and a few other valuable items.

I think we have this backward. I'd rather have alarms go off when people DON'T come to church. How much more appropriate that would be. God, I'm sure, would rather have people IN the church, than locked OUT of the church. Besides, those who would break in are those who need church the most. I hope you realize that God is alarmed when you're not in church.

Alarmingly yours,

Pastor Bob

AN EXPECTANT MOMENT

Pat and I received some wonderful news on Mother's Day. Our daughter, Rachael, and her husband, Joe, told us that they're expecting a baby. This will be our first grandchild, and needless to say, we are overjoyed! The baby's due in early January. The notion of our little girl being pregnant is exciting. Soon her belly will grow large with that new life within.

It occurs to me that "pregnant" is a good word for us as Christians. (No comments about my belly, please!) It is defined as having a new life within, and that certainly describes us in our Christian walk. We have the new life of Christ within us. He lives in our bodies as well, filling us with all sorts of new experiences, although morning sickness is not typically a common occurrence among normal church-goers. (Unless you count Sunday-morning-sickness, which afflicts those who seem to have some ailment only on Sunday mornings, which keeps them away from church.)

But "pregnant" also means "expectant." Not only do we as Christians have a new life within us, but we are expectant as well. We look forward to the coming of God's kingdom in all its glory, to the fulfillment of all God's promises. We look to the future with great anticipation, not only because of the coming birth of children and grandchildren, but because God tells us we are moving toward the culmination of all things. That probably won't happen over the course of the next nine months, but we can still live with pregnant expectation that it will happen at some point in the future.

I hope that the next time someone asks you what's new in your life, you'll respond and say: "I'm pregnant!" That'll give you a chance to explain your faith in a new way.

Pregnantly yours,

Pastor Bob

BAH! HUMBUG!

Philosopher George Berkeley raised the well-known question in his discussion of metaphysics: If a tree falls in the forest and there is no one around to witness it, will it make a sound? The issue relates to the nature of reality and perception. Can something be real if it's not perceived?

I have discovered the answer. Well, sort of. Here's my version: If a Christmas tree falls in the middle of the night, will it wake you up? The answer is yes, and it has nothing to do with metaphysics. Last night, about 4:30 a.m., our Christmas tree gave way. It's a 7-foot tall artificial tree and has a plastic stand. One of the plastic legs broke off and the whole tree went cascading into the middle of the living room. And yes, I woke up.

I, who can sleep through the worst thunder storms, tornados, and sirens, who sleeps the sleep of the dead, heard the tree go down. It wasn't a crash, really - more of a loud sigh as the branches cushioned the fall. And like the father in Clement Moore's "'Twas the Night Before Christmas," I sprang from the bed to see what was the matter. Well, crawled out of bed might be more like it.

Unfortunately, some of our favorite ornaments were broken. Pat and I tried to fix it, but at 4:30 in the morning, we're not at our best. So now the tree is relatively upright, held in place by two wires, one attached to a nail in the fireplace mantel, and one to a nail in the window casing. Oh yes, and two concrete blocks that are propping it up from underneath. I hope it'll last till New Year's Day.

So once again we are reminded that Christmas is not about trees and presents and decorations and lights and parties. It's about the miracle of Christ's birth, or God taking on human flesh and blood to become the Savior of the world. Sometimes we get so caught up in the trappings of the holiday that we forget what's really important. Pat and I have often said, "Wouldn't it be nice if we could just ignore all this other stuff and just celebrate the real meaning of Christmas?"

But here's the Biblical answer to Berkeley's question: Jesus says: "Are not two sparrows sold for a penny? Yet not one of them falls to the ground without God being aware of it. And even the hairs on your head are numbered. Are you not of more value than many sparrows?" If God is aware of sparrows that fall to the ground, I'm sure he also hears a tree when it falls, whether it's a tree in the forest, or a Christmas tree in your living room.

Coniferously yours,

Pastor Bob

I IS FOR IGNORAMUS

I have learned a new meaning for humility. I recently registered on-line to take the Jeopardy qualifying test in an effort to become a contestant on the TV quiz show. It's real easy to sit home in your comfy chair and listen to Alex Trebek give the clues to the whiz-bang contestants, and come up with the correct question yourself. Wouldn't it be fun to get on the show? Make some money? So I tried.

It's quite another matter to take the test on-line. It consisted of 50 questions that come at you, one every 15 seconds, and you have to type the correct response on the computer. I always thought I'd do fairly well. When Trivial Pursuit was all the rage I was pretty good. After all, my brain contains a vast storehouse of useless information. So I figured why not give Jeopardy a shot. BUZZ! Wrong answer!

The questions they asked were absurdly difficult

to say the least. Who was the author of contemporary best-seller Blink? What isotope of hydrogen has 1 proton and 2 neutrons? What Fauvist artist painted "Joie de Vivre?" NASA is looking for funding to study NEOs. What are NEOs? What is an 8-letter word in French for policeman? What Russian word goes with "perestroika" to denote civil relations with the West? What is the common bond between reel, hora, and habanera? Who is king of the fairies in A Midsummer Night's Dream? What activist was assassinated in San Francisco in 1978? What alloy is copper and tin? Who wrote the Alex Cross novels? Where is George Bernard Shaw's restored home? (Answers are below.)

Those are the ones I knew! The others were tougher! Some answers I thought of after the test was over. DRAT! Should have got that one. But the questions just kept coming rapid fire with no time to think in between. No commercial breaks either. If I got 25 out of 50 correct, I'd be very surprised. Ken Jennings I am not. They don't tell you how you scored, but IF you pass the test, you MAY get invited to an in-person test sometime later this year, probably in Chicago. I'm not making any plans to go to Chicago. Oh well. I can always take the test again next year, and be humiliated once again.

Fortunately, God does not require extensive knowledge of trivia. God does not give us tests, on-line or otherwise. God doesn't ask about our IQ or what degrees we have. God has merely one question to which he needs the correct answer. Who is Jesus for you? Get that one right, and you don't ever have to worry about being humbled. You don't have to worry about jeopardy or double jeopardy. You'll be the ultimate winner in God's tournament of champions.

Ignoramously yours,

Pastor Bob

Answers: Malcolm Gladwell, tritium, Matisse, near earth objects, gendarme, glasnost, dance, Oberon, Harvey Milk, bronze, James Patterson, Dublin

COUPONS ANYONE?

Do you use coupons? I think most people do, and Pat and I certainly do. We buy the big coupon book, the Super Book, every year for $39.00. It contains hundreds of coupons for everything from food at local restaurants to golf coupons to car repairs to BOGOs - Buy One Get One Free - on just about everything else. It literally pays for itself, whether you're getting a free ticket to the Civic Theatre or just going to McDonald's or Burger King.

I don't think anyone buys pizza anymore without using a coupon. I just got one today from Cottage Inn Pizza, where, I'll have you know, I am a VIP. It's good for half off my next order. They sent it to me via email in commemoration of my half-birthday. I never even knew I had a half-birthday, which is 6 months after or before your actual birthday, but if they want to give me a coupon because of it, I'll take it. It does say that the maximum value of the coupon is $25.00. So I guess if I wanted to have a big pizza party for my half-birthday, and order $50.00 worth of pizza, this would be a nice coupon to have.

The Sunday newspaper is filled with coupons. I don't mind the inserts, but I have really come to dislike those coupons that are stuck on the front page. It seems they always cover part of the headline, or part of a main story. I know you can just peel them off, but when you do, the ink comes off with them, or the paper rips. I almost want to intentionally boycott whoever that advertiser is, just because of the intrusiveness of the sticker. But Pat dutifully clips the coupons from the paper and takes them to the store when she does the grocery shopping. She has a stack of them in her wallet and generally sorts through them before she goes to the store to know which ones she has and which ones she'll be using.

There are even websites now, like Groupon, that will email coupons to your computer. And there are TV shows that feature people who save hundreds or thousands of dollars with their coupons. It's called "Extreme Couponing." One woman apparently has stockpiled 24,000 food and household items that she got for free or next-to-free simply because she used coupons. What she'll do with 24,000 such items is beyond me. Another woman bought something like $1200.00 worth of groceries and, after redeeming all her coupons, only had to pay 23 cents. Crazy!

I sometimes joke with people who don't go to church and tell them I'll give them a coupon good for free admission on Sunday morning. They don't take the coupon, but they get the idea that I'd like to see them here in church.

We all like to get something for nothing. We all like good deals, whether it's a hot sale or a high-value coupon. And it's great when the store offers double coupon day.

To top it off, if you're a senior, you sometimes get an additional discount just for being old. But the best deal of all is the one that God offers. It's totally free. Doesn't cost a nickel. It's salvation and eternal life, and all you have to do is accept it. It doesn't get any better than that.

Yours, with a 40% discount,

Pastor Bob

HEARING VOICES

I've been hearing voices lately, voices that seem to come out of nowhere. But before you think I've lost my mind completely, or that I've suddenly become like one of the Old Testament prophets, let me assure you that I remain absolutely (I think) sane.

But the other day I got on the new elevator at the hospital, and a woman's voice said: "Going up." A few moments later she said: "Third floor," which was a good thing because that's where I wanted to be. I was alone but for the voice.

We have a GPS, one of those global positioning thing-ys that gives you directions to wherever you want to go when you're driving. I won it in a drawing. (I wonder what it would say if you programmed it to give you directions to heaven. Maybe something like: "Turn right, then go straight." But that would be works-oriented salvation, wouldn't it?) This GPS actually speaks the names of the streets. So coming out of my street on the way to work, a woman who is not my wife says: "After one-quarter mile, turn right on West Main Street, semi-colon, route 43." She actually pronounces the punctuation. I don't usually need it to find my way to work or home again.

You can even choose the voice you want to hear coming out of this device. The woman's voice is the default, which means that's the one you get automatically. Or you can pay a little extra and get an English gentleman with his British accent. You can even get celebrity voices. How'd you like to hear James Earl Jones telling you how to find your way home, sounding like Darth Vader. You'd probably follow those directions accurately or expect an attack from the Death Star.

You can hear voices too. Try calling your insurance company, or your bank, or the phone company, and listen to the recorded messages telling you which button to push if you want to hear the options in Spanish, or if you want to ask about your bill, or if you need to make a claim, or want some information about your account. Usually after 45 minutes or so, you can actually get through to a live person. That voice always sounds better than all the recorded voices.

And having just come through the primary election season, with the general election still to look forward to, how about all those robo-calls? Again, it's those smooth voices that are supposed to influence us to vote for the particular candidate who paid for those calls. I tend to react just the opposite. Stop interrupting my dinner or I'll vote for the other guy or woman - the one who lets me eat in peace.

Then there are those voices from the past that come flooding into our memories. You can hear your mother's words, and the tone of voice she uses. You remember great speeches, maybe by JFK or Martin Luther King, Jr. Maybe there was a singer whose voice you loved to hear. Or maybe even a preacher? Probably not that.

Anyway the one voice we need to be listening for is that still, small voice that comes from God's Spirit. Elijah heard it, and so can we. We might be surprised by what he has to say.

Sub-vocally yours,

Pastor Bob

HELP! STUCK!

Last week Pat and I visited our grandson, Tommy. Now that he's sleeping in a big boy bed, he was proud to show us. The bed has a rail on the side to prevent him from falling out at night. He pulled us by the finger into his bedroom to proclaim that this was HIS bed.

Then he would try to climb into the bed by sticking one foot between the mattress and the box spring and throwing his other leg over the chin-high rail.

He'd only get so far and then couldn't go any further. With a grin on his face, he'd yell, "Help! Stuck! Help!"

Then we'd have to give him a little boost and flip him over the rail onto the bed, much to his delight. It was all squeals and giggles and entirely too much fun for such a simple act. Fifteen or twenty repetitions were about all we could handle, because we got tired of laughing so hard.

When Peter tried walking on water, he took his eyes off Jesus and found himself sinking into the waves. He uttered the briefest of prayers: Lord, save me! Jesus reached out his hand and flipped Peter back into the boat.

I would imagine that Jesus and the rest of the disciples had a good chuckle at Peter's misfortune. Can't you see him spluttering and fuming, wet and cold, and embarrassed?

Sometimes as we go through life, we find ourselves stuck in difficult situations. And when we do, we holler for help. It's good to know that God is there, that he hears us and is ready to lend a helping hand to get us un-stuck and where we belong.

All we need to do is cry out to God, the one Tommy called to us: Help! Stuck! Help! God will flip us to safety - over and over and over - and enjoy doing it.

One who's been flipped,

Pastor Bob

HAIR AND FAITH

As I write this, my head is cold. I don't have a cold; I just feel cold, but only on my head. You see, I just got my first haircut in Kalamazoo in 5 years. And it's short! Especially in the back - probably an inch higher on my neck than usual.

Now, I didn't go to a butcher. It was a reputable place. In fact, it was near the Western Michigan University campus, so I figured I'd get a decent haircut. College kids wouldn't tolerate bad haircuts, but my head feels cold.

The girl was nice enough. I don't even know her name, but she told me about her fiancé and her pastor and the church they attend. When she asked me how I wanted my hair cut, I was at a loss. "Short" and "long" have different meanings for different people. So I just asked for a trim and said, "Make me look respectable." Now my head is cold.

.

It's OK, I guess, because hair grows back. I'll probably even go to the same establishment the next time I need my hair cut. But as I thought about this experience, it reminded me of a couple things about our faith It's a whole lot easier to put our faith in God than it is to get a haircut from a stranger. First of all, we know who God is, and can trust him. He's no stranger to us He knows our name, our history, even the number of hairs on our head, and whether they need to be cut or not. Secondly, we believe He knows what's best for us and will see to it that we get it. That's not to say He gives us exactly what we ask for, but He does give us what's best. In fact, He knows before we even ask what it is we want and need. I also know that if God took care of my hair, my head wouldn't be cold right now.

Baldly yours,

Pastor Bob

LYRICS

"Ooh-ee-ooh-ah-ah, ting, tang, walla walla bing bang. Ooh-ee-ooh-ah-ah, ting, tang, walla walla, bing bang." Now those were good lyrics! It's the chorus from an oldie called "The Witch Doctor." We used to love those songs, didn't we? How about these: "Who put the bomp in the bomp bah bomp bah bomp? Who put the ram in the ramma lamma ding dong? Who put the bop in the bop-shoo-bop-shoo bop? Who was that man? I'd like to shake his hand. He made my baby fall in love with me. (Yeah!)...Each time that we're alone, boogity, boogity, boogity, boogity, boogity, boogity, shoo. Sets my baby's heart all aglow."

They just don't write songs like that anymore. What about "Ahab the Arab" (politically incorrect these days) who fell in love with the sultan's wife and saw her reclining in the tent with "rings on her fingers, and bells on her toes, and a bone in her nose, Ho Ho."

Or we could go back another generation to "Mairzy doats, and dozy doats, and liddle lamzy divey. A kiddley divey too, wouldn't you?" This translates to "mares eat oats and does eat oats and little lambs eat ivy. A kid will eat ivy too, wouldn't you?" Or how about: "Abba dabba dabba dabba dabba dabba dabba, said the monkey to the chimp."

Some of those old songs were pretty gruesome too. There's "Teen Angel," about a 16-year-old girl who was killed after the car stalled on the railroad tracks and she went running back to grab her boy-friend's high school ring. And then there was the song about a young lad who entered a stock car race so he could buy his girl a diamond ring with the first prize money. Unfortunately, he crashed. "And as they pulled him from the twisted wreck, with his dying breath, they heard him say, 'Tell Laura I love her. Tell Laura not to cry. My love for her will never die.'"

When we listen to the music (if you can call it that) of the younger generation, we tend to be critical of the lyrics, if we can even understand them. Yet every generation has its share of weird music and strange lyrics that drives parents and grandparents crazy.

People sometimes criticize the current trend of singing praise songs in church. They refer to them as

"7-11" music, where you sing the same 7 words 11 times over. But even some of our favorite old hymns were considered in poor taste at best. "Onward Christian Soldiers, marching as to war," is deemed overly militant. The hymns of Fanny Crosby, who wrote nearly 9,000 hymns (!), including "Blessed Assurance," "He Hideth My Soul," "Jesus Is Tenderly Calling You Home," and "Rescue the Perishing," were called sentimental, maudlin, mawkish, and saccharine.

I guess the important thing is to remember that David, one of the original lyricists, told us to "Make a joyful noise to the Lord...Come into his presence with singing."

Musically yours,

Pastor Bob

SHOP TILL YOU DROP

I think it weighed about 15 pounds, and for some folks, it was the highlight of Thanksgiving Day. Everybody had their favorite part, and there was plenty to go around. In fact, they were still into it later in the evening. The turkey? No, I'm referring to the Thanksgiving Day newspaper. The basic newspaper had 50 pages, of which 18 were an expanded classified ad section. Oh, and there was the 12-page Ticket supplement for entertainment options. Which left only 20 pages of actual news, sports, weather, obituaries, etc. But then, the real Thanksgiving Day treat - 572 pages (I actually counted them!) of holiday ad flyers from 39 different retailers.

If you were at Sam's Club at 5:00 a.m. on Friday, you could buy a guitar for $2,500 autographed by the Eagles (a rock band). Gander Mountain had a special on a Jerky Shooter with 15-lb capacity and both a flat and round nozzle for only 20 bucks. You could have purchased fine chocolates at a hardware store (Menard's) or, on Saturday, only at Big Lots, for just $50 you could be the proud owner of a 6-piece family-band outfit, including tambourine, recorder, guitar, keyboard, harmonica, and drum set. It was featured twice in their 4-page ad. Just what we all need for making beautiful music in this holiday season. I can imagine families all over Kalamazoo playing "Silent Night" on their new family-band set.

And you'd better get to bed early on Thanksgiving night. It used to be the sales started at 8:00 a.m., or maybe 7:00 a.m. on Friday morning. Then the stores began to open at 6:00 a.m. Now, 10 stores opened at 5:00 in the morning, and both Kohl's and JC Penney began the madness at 4:00 a.m. Meijer is open 24 hours a day, but the specials don't start till 5:00 a.m. Oh boy! Sleep in!

It's called Black Friday because this is the day many stores go from being unprofitable, or "in the red," to profitable or "in the black." It is one of the busiest shopping days of the year, and is traditionally considered the beginning of the Christmas shopping season, but stores have been displaying Christmas wares since right after Labor Day.

With all the hubbub surrounding Christmas, the blatant consumerism, the appeal to our materialistic and covetous nature, Black Friday seems to be the very antithesis of what took place in a stable some 2000 years ago. But I'm also reminded of another Friday - one we call Good - which was the culmination of the Incarnation. The baby born on Christmas Day died on Good Friday and rose again on Easter to provide us with eternal life. That's the real reason for this season. And you don't need to be up at 4:00 a.m. to get this best gift of all.

Jingle all the way,

Pastor Bob

YOU SMELL!

We turned the heat on in our house this week. After a week with the highs only in the 50s, it was time. You get a certain aroma in the house when the furnace kicks on for the first time in the fall.

Certain smells stir powerful memories for us. In fact, scientists tell us that odor is one of the most stimulating of the senses when it comes to helping us reminisce.

Read each item in the following list slowly. After each one, close your eyes and imagine the smell and the memories associated with it.

- newly mown grass
- burning leaves
- the fragrance of your mother's perfume (what was the name of it?)

- the musty smell in your attic when you climbed up there as a kid
- a baby, fresh from the bath, wrapped in a soft blanket
- a rose petal
- your dad's after-shave (Old Spice maybe?)
- a gardenia corsage
- lilacs in the spring
- motor oil
- a campfire
- turkey roasting in the oven
- your spouse's hair, fresh from the shower
- cigar smoke
- the smell of the salt water as you near the ocean
- cow manure in a farmer's field
- fresh-baked apple pie, hot from the oven
- a newly cut Christmas tree
- clean sheets that were dried on a clothesline, outdoors

The list could go on and on. You can add your own. Some of those smells may mean nothing to you. Others may bring back either happy or sad memories. The sense of smell can elicit some of the most powerful memories. A whiff of burning leaves may bring back a long-forgotten memory of raking in

October with your parents and siblings. A campfire may remind you of your time in the Girl Scouts, or of roasting marshmallows with your grandchildren. Widows often wear their deceased husband's old shirts because the smell brings back happy memories.

The Bible tells of certain aromas that are pleasing to God. When Noah and his family got off the ark, Noah made a burnt offering of some of the animals, and it says: "The Lord smelled the pleasing aroma." Later, when God gave Moses instructions for the tabernacle, the priests were told to burn a ram on the altar: "It is a burnt offering to the Lord, a pleasing aroma." In the New Testament, Paul wrote to the Corinthians and told them that "we are to God the aroma of Christ among those who are being saved." So you see? You smell, and I smell. We are the aroma of Christ.

Smelly me,

Pastor Bob

UNDER REPAIR

Somebody wrecked our car. Well, not wrecked really, but put a hole in it. It happened when we were on vacation in South Haven.

The car was parked in a city parking lot, and when we came out of the restaurant, there was our car with a hole in the back fender. Not just a dent, mind you. Not a little crinkle in the sheet metal or a simple ding in the paint job, but a hole about 5" in diameter!

Someone had obviously backed up into our car with a trailer hitch on the back of his car or truck and popped that baby right through our fender, leaving a jagged hole.

There were no witnesses; no one courteously left a note on our car with a name, address, and apology. Nothing. Just this gaping hole.

We got it fixed, of course. Ten days (TEN DAYS!) in the body shop and over $3300 of the insurance company's money, and the car looked good as new.

But what a nuisance it was. Having to go through the whole process with the insurance company - filling out the forms, the estimate, the revised estimate - wasn't too bad. And the body shop where the work was done was very good about their work.

But it took over 3 weeks just to schedule the work, and then another 10 days without our second car. It was downright inconvenient.

But how thankful we are for insurance. It's one of those things that you hate paying for, but are glad you've got it when you need it.

God provides us with eternal insurance. When sin knocks a hole in our lives and throws us off track, making our lives oh so inconvenient, God steps right in. He's there to make the necessary repairs, to fill the gaps, to make us even better than new. And the good thing about God's insurance? There's no deductible, no waiting for repairs, and no hassle.

Eternally insured and thankful,

Pastor Bob

WATCHING THE SIGNS

I like weather. Actually it's not just the weather I like; it's tracking the weather, watching the signs of the weather. I have a weather station at home that enables me to do all of those things. I can see the indoor and outdoor temperature, and the indoor and outdoor humidity. It tells me the wind speed and direction. I know the barometric pressure and its trend over the last 24 hours, either here in Kalamazoo, or at sea level. I can check the high and low temperatures and the high wind gust for the past 24 hours. My weather station measures the daily and annual rainfall amounts. I can use all this data to determine the wind chill and the dew point. My family thinks I'm nuts. Why not just turn on the radio for a weather forecast, or check the Weather Channel on the TV? It's all right there.

There's just something I like, though, about

doing it myself. I even keep track of it all in a little notebook. And I like comparing my own forecasts to those of Keith Thompson and his weather crew at Channel 3.

I used to have a much less sophisticated weather station. It was a rock that hung on a string. If it was wet, it was raining. If it was white, it was snowing. If it was swinging, it was windy. If it was missing, there was a tornado.

Actually, this is all very Biblical. Jesus told the Pharisees that "When it is evening, you say it will be fair weather, for the sky is red. And in the morning, it will be stormy today for the sky is red and threatening." (Matt. 16:2-3) He said to the multitudes, "When you see a cloud rising in the west, you say at once, a shower is coming; and so it happens; and when you see the south wind blowing, you will say there will be scorching heat; and it happens." (Luke 12:54-55)

Jesus is telling us to look at the signs around us - not just signs of the weather, but signs of the times. Look around at the way he blesses us. Look at the signs of a world that desperately needs a savior. Look at the opportunities he sends our way to share our faith and love with others. We don't need any elaborate weather stations to tell us of these signs. They're perfectly obvious to those with eyes to see.

The next time you see or hear a weather forecast, remember to be aware of the other signs that God is giving us.

Predictably yours,

Pastor Bob

THE PERFECT GIFT

Gifts are hard to buy. Most people these days are able to buy just about anything they need and everything they want. So when Christmas rolls around, it's hard to figure out what to get for family and friends.

It used to be that way for my parents in New York. What do you get for people who have been married for more than 60 years and are now in their 80s? My brothers and I would talk on the phone, trying to figure out what to get them. They don't really need clothes. They're not into gadgets. They don't need anything for the house. Pat and I would wrack our brains trying to come up with something.

Finally we figured it out. Each year we buy them food items for Christmas. We find unusual things they probably would never buy for themselves, packing 25 or so of them in a big box, each item individually wrapped and numbered. Over the years, the list of items has included everything from snails (escargot, for you connoisseurs), chocolate-covered coffee beans, Dutch licorice, couscous, dill mustard (my Mom can eat that right out of the jar, and often does), dark chocolate-covered cherries with liquid centers, and interestingly-flavored jelly beans.

Now they're like little kids at Christmas. They come home from church on Christmas Eve and begin opening their presents, each one in the numbered order. They sample some and save the rest to be enjoyed over the next month or two. Each time they eat something from that pack, they're reminded of us and our love for them.

My brothers are really angry at us for coming up with this novel gift idea. They still try to figure out what to buy for my folks, but Pat and I have discovered what they love to get and enjoy. It's the perfect gift for them.

It's similar to what God does for us. So many of us already have what we need and much of what we want. So in his wisdom, God gives us something we can really use and enjoy - the gift of a Savior. Each day we receive his grace and mercy. Each day we experience the forgiveness of our sin. Each day we are reminded of his love for us. It's the perfect gift - at Christmas and always. Enjoy YOUR gift this Christmas and throughout the New Year.

Giftedly,

Pastor Bob

THE EXODUS

The renowned leader gathered his people to begin the trip. A major exodus was about to begin. The people, numbering close to 2,000,000 (there were 600,000 men, plus women and children) left the land of bondage, traveled through a great wilderness, and finally reached the Promised Land.

It wasn't an easy trip, but somehow they managed to make it. Such a journey required determination, perseverance, and courage.

Along the way there were constant complaints, bickering among the family, concerns over the food, and all the other hassles that accompany such a trip. Cries of "Are we there yet?" rang out with great regularity.

Would they get lost? Would they ever reach the Promised Land? Did the leader really know what he was doing and where he was going? But the promise of the destination encouraged all those who went. They would eventually arrive at a land flowing with milk and honey, and all would be well.

I bet you thought I was referring to what Moses did with the children of Israel, leading them out of Egypt and into the land of Canaan.

Wrong! I'm writing about the mass exodus that takes place sometime between November and January when some two million of the good folks of Bethany (literary license: hyperbole) leave Michigan – the land of snow, ice, and winter bondage to travel to the Promised Land of Florida or some such warmer clime.

Good for you! I'm glad you're able to make such a journey. Take the time to enjoy God's creation along the way. Travel safely, soak up some much-needed sunshine when you get there, relax, and above all, have fun. But don't forget to come back.

Moses had nothing on Mickey Mouse.

Not a snowbird,

Pastor Bob

SWEET AND SOUR THANKSGIVING

I really don't like cranberry sauce. I know it's traditional at Thanksgiving to have cranberry sauce or cranberry jelly or cranberry relish with the turkey, but I don't care for any of them.

I won't say I hate cranberries, because I suppose one shouldn't hate any food that God has provided (see, I'm remembering my own sermon from a couple weeks ago about Peter's vision and the sheet that came down from heaven with all the different non-kosher foods), but I dislike them intensely. How's that?

I think the reason is that somehow cranberries combine the sweet and tart tastes in a way that doesn't do much for me. I like Sweet-Tarts, those little pastel-colored candies that come in a roll and melt in your mouth if you don't chew them up first. But they're more sweet than tart. And I like sweet and sour sauce at the Chinese restaurants. But there's something about that combination at the Thanksgiving table that just doesn't sit right with me. Cranberries are too sweet and too tart to go with any of the other foods. So pass the turkey, the mashed potatoes, the dressing, and the gravy, but forget the cranberries.

Actually, there's more sweet and sour at our Thanksgiving tables than the cranberries. Thanksgiving is probably the biggest family holiday of all. It's the one time that families gather just to be together, with no ulterior motives of getting gifts, like at Christmas, or candy, like at Easter. There's a sweet joy about just being together and giving thanks for all God has given us.

But there's also a tart side to many Thanksgiving celebrations. For many, it's a difficult time because part of the family isn't there. Perhaps there was a death that has taken a loved one from this family to his or her heavenly family. For others, it's a broken home, a shattered relationship, or just a result of distance. Whatever the reason, there's often a part of Thanksgiving that makes it a hard holiday to endure.

But when we give thanks, it is sweet music to God's ears. May you focus on the sweetness of the holiday, and may the tart and sour aspects be minimized.

Thankfully yours,

Pastor Bob

WHICH BUTTON
DO I PUSH?

A couple of weeks ago, our garage door broke. Actually, it wasn't the garage door itself, not the big spring that sometimes snaps and scares you out of your skin. This time it was the motor that opens the door when you push the button on the remote control unit in your car. So for a week or so, whenever I wanted to get the car out of the garage or put the car into the garage, I had to manually open the door. That's not really a big deal, just an inconvenience.

It got me thinking about remote control devices. They have become omnipresent in our lives, and we tend to take them for granted. It used to be we had to get up from our chairs to change the channel on the TV. My grandfather didn't like doing that all the time, so he put one channel on and left it on all day, unless one of us grandkids were there, and then he'd bribe us with a nickel to change the channel for him. When I was a kid, my dad would say, "Go change the channel," and I had to get up off the floor and go to the actual television set and turn a knob that changed the channel. My dad didn't have to do it, so I guess I was his "remote control." Have we become so sedentary that we can't get out of our La-Z-Boys to change the channel on the TV set? Well, why bother, when we have remote controls?

How many remote controls do you have in your home? I counted about 117 in our house. We've got remote controls for the TV sets, remote controls for the cable boxes, remotes controls for the garage door openers, a remote control for the gas fireplace, remote controls for the sound system, remote controls for the DVD players, remote controls for the grandkids' toys, and some remote controls that I don't even know what they're for. I even have a remote control for my camera that allows me to snap a picture from across the room. That's handy for when I want to be in the picture myself. Just put the camera on a tripod, focus the camera, hustle into the picture, push the remote button, and BINGO! The remote releases the shutter, and I'm in the picture. Some people even have remote controls that start their car for them! We may even have remote controls for the remote controls. You know, push the button on one remote and the other remote control comes on.

You can buy all kinds of remotes, including some that are advertised as "universal remotes." They're supposed to work for every device you've got. They cost anywhere from $10 to $120. When Pat's mom lived with us, she had a collection of remotes. One was for the TV, one for the cable box, one for the CD player on her little boom box, and one for the gas fireplace insert. With that remote, she could make the flame come on, then raise or lower it to her preferred level. She could adjust the fan speed, and set the actual temperature she wanted in the room. One year, one of Pat's brothers thought it would be nice to give her one of those universal remotes for Christmas. It's supposed to work for everything. It didn't. In fact, although I was able to program it for the TV, it didn't work for the cable box or for her fireplace or for her boom box. So there it sits, just one more lonely remote that controls nothing.

They sell remote control caddies, handy little things with pouches that store anywhere from 4 to 6 remote controls devices. You can buy remotes with extra large buttons for the visually impaired.

My folks had one remote for the TV, one for the combination DVD-VCR and then they each had a universal remote that only controlled the channel selection and volume for the TV. They could have had battling remotes, I suppose, each of them using their personal remote to decide what they were going to watch on TV. That would've been fun to watch. Dueling remotes. My mom would have won I think.

One of my remotes has 52 buttons, and another one has 48. Between the 2, that's 100 buttons. I have no idea what they're all for. Some are for volume, some change the channel, some give you information about the program, and one brings up a TV guide thing-y that shows a grid with all the different programs and what time they come on. They ought to make a special remote for the technologically challenged with 3 buttons - on/off, channel up/down, and volume up/down. I suppose I could figure out what all those different buttons are for, but I'd have to read the instruction manual, but the only way to get it is to use the remote to access the instruction manual on your TV. I don't know how to do that. I tried pushing some of the buttons on my remote, but they didn't seem to do anything. With others, I got a message that said, "This function currently disabled."

Have you ever wondered how these things work? There's an infrared signal that shoots out from the front of the remote that is picked up by a receiver on the unit to be controlled. They must use different frequencies so the DVD player doesn't get turned on when you want to lower the volume on the TV.

Somebody actually got smart and eliminated the need for remotes, at least to some extent. Now there's a remote you can use to simply speak your preference. Voice activated TVs. Tell the remote what program you're looking for, and it will find it for you. Tell the remote to turn the volume up, and it gets louder. When the phone rings, you can use your remote to turn the volume down, or to pause the program while you answer the phone. Or when you see on the TV screen who it is that's calling you, you can ignore the phone altogether.

Thankfully, we don't need a remote control for God. He's there for us at all times and in all places. He's never OFF; he's always ON. We don't need to figure out what button to push to get his attention. And God is voice-activated. A simple prayer will suffice. In fact, all we need to do is think something and God knows it. And it's a good thing, too. As technologically challenged as most of us are, we'd never get through otherwise. Now if we could just get our TVs to be more like God....

Remotely yours,

Pastor Bob

OF MICE AND CARS

Pat's car smells. Actually, last week she told me her car had a bad aroma after it warmed up. As any good mechanic knows, this indicates serious trouble. Being the outstanding mechanic that I am, I got the car out, ran it around the block a few times, and started sniffing around. Sure enough, it smelled bad. This means you need to check the engine, which I proceeded to do. Opening the hood, I immediately discovered the source of the problem. Pat's car smelled bad because our dog has allergies!

This is not as far-fetched as it sounds. Let me explain. Our dog used to eat a lamb-based dry dog food. He got ear infections and dandruff, and the vet said it was because he's allergic to lamb. That meant we had to get a new dog food. The old lamb-based food was put into the garage, to be given to a non-allergic dog at some point. In the winter, mice come into the garage, wisely getting out of the cold weather. Sensing the presence of this wonderful lamb dog food, they nibbled their way through the bag and into the feast itself. Worried that some ogre would come along and remove this source of their dining pleasure, the mice decided to store some extra pellets where no one would find it. Little did they know the extent of my mechanical expertise. The dog food was carefully stashed on the warm engine of Pat's car, nestled into every nook and cranny available. So when the car warmed up, Pat was cooking lamb dog food, and the aroma, admittedly, was less than appealing.

Several lessons leap out at me from this experience:

1. First of all, isn't it amazing that God made mice with such discriminating tastes?
2. We think ants are industrious, but what about mice? Can you imagine these mice making a trip from one corner of the garage where the dog food was kept, all the way across the garage, then up into the engine housing of Pat's car? They must have made lots of trips. I wonder how long it took. And how many mice actually were involved. A couple? A family? A clan? A mouse couldn't possible carry more than one pellet at

a time, and I removed over 40 of them. Or did they have a pellet brigade - a whole line of mice passing a pellet from one to the other until each one was nicely stowed in the manifold? Did we ever interrupt them in their labors? Did opening the garage door signal them to run for cover? Did they get real disappointed when Pat drove her car away, taking with her their hidden stash of food? I just have a lot of questions here.

3. Thirdly, not everything that smells bad is as tragic as you initially think. A little investigation will often reveal that what we assume to be a major difficulty is nothing more than a minor inconvenience.

4. Fourth, sometimes the source of our problems is not what we think it is. This is true for all of life. Maybe it's not the fault of carmakers who build unreliable cars, or God's fault for making those pesky mice. Maybe it's the fault of the stupid (sinful?) person who left the dog food in the garage in the first place.

Mechanically yours,

Pastor Bob

HOLE-Y, HOLE-Y, HOLE-Y!

We have a hole in our yard, right in the front yard. It's 8 feet long, 5 feet wide, and 6 feet deep. It's a big hole. Last Friday, one of our neighbors smelled gas and called Consumers Energy. On Friday evening, one of their workers was wandering around the neighborhood with a little device he called a sniffer. It checks for gas leaks by detecting the relative strength of the aroma. Natural gas has a special chemical added to it that gives it that "rotten egg" smell, just so we can tell if there's a leak someplace. Ordinarily, it has no odor at all.

Anyway, the man's sniffer told him there was a gas leak in the line that led to our neighbor's house across the street, and that they'd have to dig up the line to repair it. A backhoe was brought in along with two or three Consumers' trucks, a digging crew, and a least one supervisor. Overtime, you know.

By 9:00 that evening, we had ourselves a big hole. The main gas line runs under our front yard (aren't we lucky?), and it's from there that each house has a line running to it. The leak was at the "T" connection where the neighbor's line attached to the main line. That meant they had to dig to the main line - in our yard.

Now a backhoe is no small piece of equipment. It's like a bulldozer with a digging claw on one end. It weighs somewhere around 13,547 tons, and has huge treads on it like an army tank. It does not do nice things to your lawn.

Our front lawn isn't anything great, but it usually looks pretty good. I put fertilizer and weed killer on it, and I keep it nicely mowed. But now it is scarred with a large hole and tread marks from the backhoe. It's chewed up and dug up, and generally a mess. Plus, there's this huge pile of dirt that came out of the hole, and there are barricades and orange cones to warn people to steer clear. The workers assure me that everything will be put back to its prior condition. Right.

By the time you read this, I'm sure our hole will be filled in and the pile of dirt will be gone and the barricades and workers will have gone to some other leaky gas line. But in the meantime, I'll have some work to do to repair the front yard.

All this reminds me that sometimes one person has to put up with an inconvenience or a cost so that someone else can be OK. We had to put up with a torn-up yard so our neighbors could have gas for their furnace, even though we had no leak. If one of our trees fell on a neighbor's house, we'd have to pay to have the tree removed even though there was no damage to our house.

God pays a price so that we can be OK in our spiritual lives. He sacrificed his only son, Jesus, so that we could receive eternal life. The holes that sin put in our lives have been completely filled in. God paid a debt that he didn't owe because we owed a debt that we couldn't pay. And the price that God paid was infinitely higher than anything I'll have to pay to fix my lawn.

Yours with a shovel, rake, hoe, and grass seed,
And with my sins forgiven,

Pastor Bob

NEW-FANGLED PHONES

A couple of weeks ago I was in another office and asked if I could make a phone call. It was no problem; there was a phone on an end table next to the couch where I was sitting. As I picked up the receiver I suddenly realized that it was a dial phone - one of those old-fashioned kind with an actual dial - a round thing with 10 holes in it.

You can't imagine how strange it felt to stick my finger in each hole as I was dialing the number and then waiting for the dial to return to its original position for the next number. I'm told that today's younger generation has no clue how to use one of these phones. They poke it and prod it, never thinking that they have to stick their finger in the number hole and twist the dial around.

But it got me thinking about how phones have changed over time. Phones used to have a handle that you cranked, which rang an operator - a real live person - who then put your call through on a switchboard. When I was a kid, our phone number only had 4 digits (1534). And we had a party line, which meant that there were 3 families in whose houses the phones were all connected. If you wanted to make a call, you had to make sure one of your neighbors wasn't using their phone, because then you'd have to wait until they were through. It also meant they could listen in to your calls, and we had one nosy neighbor who used to do that.

Then our phone number went to 5 digits (3-1534) and then they added a fancy exchange - ours was TWINBROOK, which was shortened to the first 2 letters followed by 5 numbers. But then they also changed the digits, so our new number was TW5-2146, or numerically, it was 895-2146. Then they added a 3-digit area code. You needed to remember 10 digits for your own phone number. And if you were dialing someone outside your area code, you had to add a 1 in front of the other 10 numbers.

Phones now are actually computers that you carry around in your pocket. They have screens that tell you who is calling before you even answer it. You put in a list of contacts with all their pertinent information, so you don't need to remember phone numbers anymore. In fact, you can just tell your smart phone to "Call home," or whoever, and it happens. In fact you don't even have to call. You can text, which means typing the words of your message on a keyboard smaller than a matchbook (who even knows what a matchbook is anymore?) and it gets sent to the other person's smart phone. With some phones you can just speak your "text" and it gets typed out for you.

And today's smart phones are much more than phones. They have cameras so that you can snap a picture then email it to your friends all around the world. You can check your email. You can set the alarm to wake you in the morning. You can access the internet. You can read books that you've downloaded from the library or from Amazon. They are calculators and pedometers. These devices act as translators. You can translate from 103 different languages, either written or spoken, into English, and from English into any of those 103 different languages. You can listen to music that you've downloaded from the world-wide-web. They record your daily schedule and remind you of upcoming appointments and important dates. You can use them as a GPS, allowing them to give you directions to wherever you want to go. You can access the local weather conditions including the radar. You can use them to pay at the grocery store or coffee shop. You can even send money to friends if you need to pay them back some money you borrowed from them or if you lost a bet on the big game. You can access amazon.com and buy anything your heart desires from anywhere in the world. You can unlock your front door, make sure your garage door is closed, start your car before you get there, and adjust the thermostat in your house while on your way home. You can watch TV or movies on your smart phone. And have you noticed that the younger generation never wears a watch anymore? If you ask them the time, they simply glance at their phone. You can even make a phone call!

I remember going to the World's Fair in New York City in 1964 and being amazed by AT&T's exhibit of a "video-phone," where you could actually see the person you were speaking to. What was the world coming to? This too has become commonplace with FaceTime on your phone or iPad.

The communicators of Star Trek and Dick Tracy's wrist-radios are today's reality. I wonder where the next 20 years will take us in the area of interpersonal communication. Right now, we've lost some of the "interpersonal" part, as you can sometimes see two people sitting in a booth in a restaurant texting each other on their phones instead of looking up and actually speaking to one another.

I used to be something of a Luddite. For those of you unfamiliar with the term, the Luddites were a group of masked men in Britain from 1811 to 1816 who rioted and destroyed machinery, usually machines that were used in the textile industry, because they believed this new technology threatened jobs.

In contemporary times, a Luddite is someone who dislikes and often rejects modern technology. I resisted getting a cell phone for years, saying I didn't want to be that available. Then we got one that we only used when we traveled. It was for emergencies and for making hotel reservations, or for notifying family when we expected to arrive.

I've finally succumbed. I have a smart phone. I still use it mainly for traveling and for emergencies. But it's also nice for asking my Google Assistant what movies are playing at the local theater, or for checking the menu at a new restaurant, or for discovering how old a certain actor is. I can also find out how many miles it is from Boise, Idaho to Juneau, Alaska. (2,142 miles) And I now know that the cube root of 4672 is approximately 16.7173567855.

Thankfully God's forms of communication have not changed. He continues to speak to us through his word, through the words and actions of other people, and in our prayer times. We don't need high-tech devices to get in touch with God. We're never out of range and the lines are never busy. The circuits to God are never overloaded. He's only a breath away and you'll never be disconnected. He never puts you on hold and there's no call waiting. God offers us the original "Direct Connect." It doesn't get any better than that.

Telephonically yours,

Pastor Bob

OUT OF CONTROL

When I was in the hospital a couple of weeks ago, I learned a powerful lesson. It happened about 12:15 a.m. I was absolutely exhausted and had fallen asleep only a short time before because of all the wires and the IV needle and the heart monitor and everything else that they keep you plugged into. Trying to sleep when you're in a hospital bed shaped like a dugout canoe is not easy. It felt soooo good to finally get to sleep.

Anyway, this dear woman appeared at my bedside to take my vital signs - blood pressure, with the cuff squeezing your arm till it feels like it's going to drop off; temperature - under your tongue, not in your ear; heart rate; respiration - all of it. I endured these inconveniences with only a moderate degree of annoyance, hoping she'd soon be through and I could go back to sleep.

But then she told me I had to get out of bed and stand on a scale so she could record my weight. This was the last thing I wanted to do at that hour of the morning. They had just weighed me at 4:00 that afternoon. I hadn't eaten a thing. I assured her that I didn't weigh more than half a pound different from what I weighed just 8 hours earlier, and I could tell her what my weight was, either in pounds or kilograms. Why couldn't she just go away and let me sleep?

No way, she said. Either I got up and got weighed then and there, or she'd be back at 5:30 a.m. and get my weight then before she finished her shift. What a bully!

Now, I understand why they have to weigh you all the time. It's not because they're checking on the efficacy of hospital food diets. It's because they need to know if you're retaining water. But all I wanted to do was sleep!

By the time I went through my arguments with her, I decided I might just as well get up and stand on the scale. I was right too. I weighed three-tenths of a pound less.

Now here's the lesson: there are times when you can be in control of your life, and times when you can't. As much as we'd like to be in control all the time, it's impossible. This hospital employee let me know that, and I acquiesced.

The same is true with our spiritual lives. We can't be in control all the time, and we shouldn't be. Sometimes we just need to let go and let God take charge. The fact is, he's better at running things than we are anyway. It's just so hard to let go. Our lives would be so much easier if we let him be in control all the time.

Patient-ly yours,

Pastor Bob

PAYING THE PRICE

I ignored the warnings and I paid the price. When will I learn? Last week, driving home from New York where I visited with my parents, I was driving on the interstate highway when I saw one of those flashing lights that said: When flashing, turn to 1640 AM for highway information.

I turned on the radio to that station and heard that there had been an accident on I-80 westbound, the route I was planning to take. The radio announcement from Penn-DOT, the Pennsylvania Department of Transportation, said a vehicle had caught fire at 5:00 a.m. and that traffic was being rerouted around the accident site. They suggested an alternate route.

It was then about 10:00 in the morning. Surely, I thought, the fire would be extinguished by now. Certainly, there would be clear sailing some five hours after the accident happened. So I ignored the warning on the radio.

I got onto I-80 about 15 miles from where they said the accident happened. No problems. The traffic was sailing along at 70 mph or better. "Ah, just as I thought. I'm glad I didn't get off the highway and start working my way through the mountains on those narrow two-lane roads with all the semis creeping along at 20 mph."

My reverie and self-satisfied smugness lasted all of 10 minutes. Shortly after I passed the exit where they suggested all traffic get off the highway, I came to a screeching halt. And there I sat. For nearly an hour and a half I inched my way along for that last five miles until I reached the point where the accident happened.

It seems a huge truck loaded with garbage had sailed through the guard rail and crashed into the side of the mountain. It tipped over, spilling its load, and caught fire. Trash was all over the road. There were front-end loaders trying to clean up the mess. Fire trucks, tow trucks, and police cars were every-where - still. And I crept along, moving one or two car lengths at a time until I got past the site. Why did I ignore the warning? It was perfectly clear and accurate. But I paid the price with a long delay.

Isn't that often the case in all of life? There are warnings for us every day. God says, "Don't go that way. Turn around. Take an alternate route." And in our "wisdom" we say, "What does God know? I can go my way and not have to worry." And how often do we pay the price? How often do we find ourselves stuck? All too often, I'm afraid.

But then we read this, or something close to it: "There is a way which seems right to a man, but its end is the way to traffic jams." (Proverbs 14:12) And again, "Yea though I drive through the traffic jams of life, I will fear no evil, for God is with me." (Psalm 23:4) No matter how stuck we find ourselves, God does not leave us to the detours of life.

All jammed up,

Pastor Bob

NICKNAMES

People call me Twig. It's my nickname, a variation on Terwilliger. I suspect that just about every Terwilliger has been called Twig at some time in his or her life. My Dad was. My son is. Wayne Terwilliger, the old-time professional baseball player still is. I have his baseball card from 1957, and it says he was called Twig. And I am too.

Most people here at Bethany call me Pastor Bob. That's sort of a nickname. It combines familiarity with a level of respect. I like it. But other folks here still call me Twig. Often on the golf course, that's what some people call me. But even on the golf course, there are those folks who still refer to me as "Pastor Bob." Am I a pastor on the golf course? I guess so.

Most people have nicknames. Maybe it was something your parents called you. Or maybe you need to look back into your high school yearbook to see what your nickname was then, what your classmates called you.

Our grandson William, when he was 3 announced to us that he wanted to be called Scooter. But now he's just William again. Sometimes we need to try out nicknames to see what we like.

Many nicknames are simply shortened forms of our given name. Bob is short for Robert. Jim is short for James. Pat is short for Patricia or Patrick. That's OK, but they don't have the same ring as special nicknames like Tiger or Ol' Blue Eyes or Rocky. Other times, we just use terms of endearment. I refer to my wife as "Pat" when I'm talking about her to other people. But I seldom address her that way when speaking directly to her. It's usually "Honey," or "Hon," or some variation.

When I first came to Kalamazoo, a good friend and colleague was (Rev.) Charlie Cohagen. He always referred to his wife as "Honey," even when talking about her in the third person. For years, I assumed that was her given name. It's not. Imagine my embarrassment when, after calling her "Honey" for nearly 10 years, I learned that her name is Joanne. Oops!

Names are important in the Bible. Sometimes a name reveals something about a person's character, like Peter, the Rock, or about their history, like Israel (formerly Jacob), which means "He who strives with God." We are told not to take the Lord's name in vain. When we baptize, we do it in the name of the Father and the Son and the Holy Spirit. We pray in Jesus' name.

In Isaiah, God says he has inscribed our name on the palm of his hand. But most importantly, we're told that our names have been written in the Lamb's Book of Life. It doesn't matter what you're called on earth, as long as your name is shouted out in that final roll call in heaven.

My name is,

Twig, or *Pastor Bob*

ROCKS

Driving through the mountains in Pennsylvania this past week, I went past a sign that said: "Watch for fallen rocks." That got me thinking about rocks. They're really interesting because there are all kinds of rocks - big ones, small ones, oddly-shaped ones. There are igneous, sedimentary, and metamorphic rocks. Fascinating things. The smallest ones are called pebbles; bigger ones are called stones. Larger ones are called rocks, and then there are boulders. Anything bigger than a boulder is a mountain, I guess.

Some people have rock gardens, but I don't think they ever grow, even if you water them and fertilize them. Some people actually collect rocks. You can buy a special tumbler that you put the rocks in with some grit and, after a few weeks, the rocks are polished.

I have a couple rocks that I've picked up over the years. I'm not sure why I save them, except they look kind of cool. And some of you have Petoskey stones, the state rock of Michigan, the fossilized coral you can find along the shores of Lake Michigan. Some of you may have a geode, which looks ordinary on the outside, but has crystals on the inside when it's split open. Some people are like that - ordinary on the outside, but absolutely beautiful on the inside.

Some rocks are really valuable, especially those we call diamonds, emeralds, sapphires, rubies, and other gemstones. We all know people who are real gems, too.

Rocky is a good name. My folks once had a dog named Rocky, but you can probably think of people with that name. Boxers are often called Rocky. There's Rocky Marciano, Rocky Graziano, and Rocky Balboa. And if you understand that the name "Peter" means "Rock," then he could have been called Rocky too, as in *The Cotton Patch Gospel*. Maybe Peter was a fallen rock, at least when he denied knowing Jesus.

Some drinks are ordered "on the rocks," meaning over ice, which is rocky water, I guess. And then there are the musical references. You've got rock and roll, hard rock, soft rock, acid rock, and classical rock.

But my favorite rock of all is one that is seldom noticed and rarely referred to, except maybe once a year on Easter morning. That's the rock that was used to cover the grave of Jesus after his crucifixion. Remember that Joseph of Arimathea took Jesus' body, wrapped it in a clean linen cloth, and placed it in his own tomb. A big stone was rolled in front of the entrance, and later, Pilate, afraid that someone would steal the body and claim that Jesus had risen from the dead, had a seal placed on the stone, and set guards outside the tomb.

On Easter morning, as the women were going to the tomb to anoint Jesus' body, they wondered who was going to roll away that stone. Matthew tells us that an angel had already taken care of that task.

So I really like this rock. It represents God's action on Easter Sunday, not by allowing Jesus to get out of the grave, but allowing the women, and later the disciples, to get IN and discover the wonderful news that Jesus was alive. May God roll away all the rocks in your life, and allow you to experience the wonder and awe of the resurrection for yourself.

Stonily yours,

Pastor Bob

SELF-SERVICE

Have you noticed that we now live in a self-service world? Society has changed so much that service by others has become largely a thing of the past, or, if you do happen to find it, a rarity. It used to be you'd pull into a gas station and a cheerful attendant would come bouncing out as your rolled your window down, and asked, "What'll it be?" "Fill 'er up," you'd reply, as you reached into your wallet for $3.00, wondering if you might need another fifty cents or so. While the gasoline went into your tank, the attendant would wash your windshield and check your oil. If he was good, he'd wash your rear window as well.

Now, you pull into a gas station, get out of your car, regardless of the weather, punch some buttons on the gas pump, then realize that you have to pay first. So you run into the station, wondering if your

$50 bill will cover it, then go back, unscrew your gas cap, put the pump in, wash your own windshield while the gas is flowing, pull out the pump when your tank is full, and proceed to spill gas all over your new shoes as you figure out how to replace the silly nozzle. And check the oil? No way.

It used to be you'd go to the bank with your paycheck, and speak to a friendly teller who knew your name, and would deposit part of your check, and give you some cash back. Now our checks are deposited automatically into our accounts and you go to an ATM to get whatever cash you need. Who needs tellers?

You used to go into a restaurant, be seated by a hostess, and have some perky waitress take your order, serve your food, clean away the dishes when you were done, and carry on a pleasant conversation through the meal. Now you seat yourself and go to a buffet where the plates are at one end; you dish up your own food (going back as many times as you like, of course), and leave when you're done. Oh, you can even make yourself a soft-serve ice cream cone for dessert.

In the grocery store, there used to be check-out persons and baggers, and at some stores, young people who would even carry your groceries to the car. Now you scan the items yourself, bag them yourself, and lug them yourself. You don't even have to give your money to a real person. Just stick it in the slot, take your change and your receipt, and don't forget to take your items with you. (Who would ever forget to take the items? That's why you're in the store in the first place.)

Thankfully, we haven't yet reached the point where we have self-serve dentistry or self-serve surgery. And I don't think we have self-serve church. In fact, it's just the opposite: we are called on by God to serve others. And thankfully, we don't have a God who, when we pray and ask for something, says: "Get it yourself!" He takes care of us, giving us more than we need, more than we ask for, and more than we deserve.

Serving God, and serving you, even as I serve myself,

Pastor Bob

HARD TO GET INTO

Do you ever have trouble opening packages? I know I do, and my wife certainly does. You buy a package of over-the-counter medicine, and it's in a child-proof package. First you wrestle with the box it comes in. You finally get it open, and the bottle inside has a plastic wrapper around the lid. You get that off and then you have to deal with the child-proof cap. You push and twist and lift and maybe you can get it open. But more often than not, you have to find a kid to open it for you. So much for "child-proof."

Finally, the lid is off and there's a foil cover over the mouth of the bottle, which you think you can easily puncture with your finger nail. Not true. You push down and all it does is stretch a little bit. Finally you get a knife and puncture the foil, but can you get the pills out yet?

NOOOO... There's a whole bale of cotton stuffed

inside the bottle and over the pills. Do you think I can get my finger in there to get that cotton out? Unh-uh. So then you go find some tweezers to reach in and get the cotton out, but it rips and shreds and you have to work at it for several minutes.

By the time the pills are accessible, you've forgotten why you needed them anyway. Or maybe your headache has become so painful from trying to get at the pills, you just go directly to the emergency room. I can hear it now: The doctor says, "Why are you here at the hospital?" And you reply: "Because I couldn't open the bottle of pills for my headache."

And it's not just medicine that's packed that way. How do you open a box of crackers or cereal? Can you just lift the flap on the box without ripping it all the way down the side? So much for those easy-open, easy-close tops. And then, you've got to get into the waxed paper bag on the inside.

Wouldn't it be nice if they just zipped open? You try to very carefully pull the sides of the bag apart so you don't rip the bag, but before you know it, the whole bag is ripped and the cereal or crackers are all over the place.

And what about a bag of potato chips? You might just as well rip it open with your teeth and throw the potato chips all over the kitchen floor to begin with. That's where they end up anyway. And forget about resealing that bag.

Ah, the wonders of modern packaging. Why do they make things so hard to get into?

That's made me wonder about the church. Is the church hard to get into? I know we need to be aware of folks with disabilities who might have a tough time navigating icy parking lots and flights of stairs, so we need to make sure the church is physically accessible and safely so. But what about other hindrances? Are there barriers to people being accepted in the church? Things like skin color, national background, gender or sexual orientation? Do we make visitors feel uncomfortable when they come? Are there requirements that make it difficult to get in here?

God says that all the walls have to come down, that the doors need to be thrown open wide. The church must be the easiest place to get into so everyone can experience the magnificent love and grace that God offers.

Your packaging guru,

Pastor Bob

SLEEPY TIME

When my wife and I travel, we often spend the night at a Holiday Inn Express. They have reasonable rates, they're well-located near major highways, almost all have indoor pools and sometimes hot tubs that can ease your weary bones after a day in the car. They have mini-fridges and coffee makers in the rooms, and they all offer free hot breakfast in the morning. That alone makes the stay worthwhile. You can have a hearty breakfast of eggs, sausage or bacon, cereal, sometimes waffles or pancakes, cinnamon rolls, fresh fruit, your choice of several juices, and hot coffee. With that in your stomach, lunch becomes an often avoidable option.

On this last trip, we stopped for the evening at one such Inn. We were pleased to note that they had recently undergone a major renovation. Sure enough we could see there was new carpeting in the halls and in the rooms, and there was fresh paint on the walls. In fact the stairways were still being painted and we had to use the elevator exclusively. Once in the room we noticed a small placard that indicated they had new beds. "You'll sleep in comfort tonight in our new beds!" it proclaimed.

When it was time for bed, I immediately noticed that the bed was quite high off the floor. With the new 16" mattress and the new 16" bedsprings, and the 12" or 15" base, and the 3 or 4 inches of down comforters piled on top, the bed was easily 4 feet off the ground. Now, four feet is considerably higher than where my sitter is, meaning I couldn't just back up and sit down on the edge of the bed. In fact, when I backed up, the top of the bed was in the small of my back. Imagine how much more difficult it was for my 5'4" wife.

Nor could I get into bed by standing sideways next to it and throwing one leg up as if I were mounting a horse. Even if I could get my leg that high, there was nothing to grab onto, no saddle with a horn to pull myself up. In fact, even thinking about such a maneuver caused me to pull a muscle.

Noting the lack of a stepladder in the room, I quickly ascertained that I would have to resort to a high jump of Olympic proportions. I backed up a few steps, picked up momentum, and made a mighty leap, only to land short of the middle of the bed. I quickly slid to the floor, pulling the down comforters on top of me, while my wife laughed herself silly.

A second effort proved successful, and from my elevated perch, I was able to pull my wife onto the bed. Once there, neither one of us was sure if we wanted to remain there, not because we were afraid of falling out of bed, but because this sumptuous new bed was so soft it was like laying in a bowl of mashed potatoes. We sank deep into the clouds of pillow-top "comfort," and almost couldn't get out of this deep pit into which we were nearly swallowed. First we couldn't get into bed, and now we couldn't get out.

I guess we should be thankful. Jesus reminds us that "the birds have nests and the foxes have holes, but the Son of Man has nowhere to lay his head." And remember, when Jacob was returning to his brother Esau to make amends after stealing his birthright, he spent the night before that meeting sleeping with a rock for a pillow.

At least we got a hot breakfast out of it.

Sleepily Yours,

Pastor Bob

HELLO, MY NAME IS...

It's 6 a.m. and I'm sitting in the Outpatient Surgery Waiting Room at Bronson Hospital. Sebastian is here for his knee replacement, and I'm waiting to go back to the pre-op area so I can pray with him before the surgery. It's crowded today I count 37 folks either waiting for surgery, or waiting for a family member or friend who is having surgery.

Sharon B. sits behind the desk. She signs people in and keeps track of family members, so when the nurse comes out to take a patient in, or when a doctor comes out to speak to the family, she directs them to the right person. She's been doing this for 13 ½ years, and is excellent at her job, maybe even infallible.

I asked her this morning how she can remember what can sometimes be 40 or 50 people in the waiting room. How does she remember the names?

On her list of patients, she makes little notes. She indicates where in the room people sit, the first names of all family members (no last names are allowed because of the HIPPA privacy laws), and what color clothes they're wearing. She also records cell phone numbers in case the family leaves the area.

I like to think I'm halfway decent at remembering names. I think it's important for folks who come to church to be greeted by name and to feel like they belong, like they're important enough to be remembered.

One of the benefits of a smaller church is that it's possible to do that. Visitors and infrequent attenders can be easily ignored and overlooked in a crowd of 1000 or 1500 in the larger churches, but not so easily here at Bethany.

Some say the easiest way to remember a name is to make an association between the name and some aspect of the person. You have to be careful doing that. One apocryphal story tells of a minister who wanted to remember a rather portly visitor, Mr. Franklin, by name, so he remembered that Benjamin Franklin invented the pot-belly stove and bifocals, which this gentleman wore. The only problem was that the next Sunday, as Mr. Franklin came through the greeting line after church, the minister, remembering the association, said, "Good Morning, Mr. Potbelly!" Not good.

We have a God who not only remembers our names, but who cares deeply about each one of us. In Isaiah 49:16, God says: "Look, I've written your names on the palms of my hands." So that's how he does it, that's how he remembers our names! And I thought it was just because we always sit in the same pew every week.

My name is,

Pastor Bob

And God knows it!

IMPRINT OF
THE SPIRIT

I'm not sure if you noticed or not, but there are three windows at church where pigeons have left an imprint. It's not what you think. They've actually flown into the glass and left the image of their heads, bodies, wings, and even the beak. One is especially prominent, on the window by the elevator entrance off the parking lot. You can even see individual wing feathers. The other two are above the north entry doors, one on the west side, and another, almost like a partner, on the east side.

I understand that birds do this because they see the reflection of trees and clouds in the window and think they're just flying off into the wild blue yonder, and SMACK! into the glass they go. Pigeons must be dirty birds because when they hit the window, they leave quite an image. I assume it's the dirt and dust from their feathers

Now you may think this is a sign that we have especially clean windows in the church, which we do. It may also mean that the church is frequented by stupid pigeons, which is probably also true. But I also think it's a sign from God.

You've all see the sign of the dove, a symbol of the Holy Spirit. These pigeon imprints look like signs of the dove. I think it's God's way of putting his stamp of approval on Bethany. I look at those windows and smile, because it says to me that God is blessing us. We see it on Sunday morning in worship. We see it in our weekday activities as we reach out to the neighborhood. And now we can look at our windows and see visible signs of the Spirit as well. In fact, we can see signs of God's blessings all around us. All we need to do is look.

Ornith-theologically yours,

Pastor Bob

SPIRITUAL SURGERY

I learned a new word this past month That's not all that unusual because I learn lots of new words all the time. I love crossword puzzles and that pastime constantly stretches my vocabulary. But this word has a medical meaning with what I consider spiritual overtones. The word is "debridement." It's pronounced "dee-breed-meant." It refers to the surgical removal of unhealthy, lacerated, or devitalized tissue. It's what Dr. Halpern did to my knee. He took what he called a scope and went into my knee joint through 3 small holes and scraped away all the bad, dead tissue that was causing so much pain. He had to smooth out a "bucket-handle tear" (a tear that looks like the handle of a bucket, sort of semicircular) in the cartilage between my femur (thigh bone), and my tibia (shin bone). Ultimately he says I'll need a knee replacement. And it's because he did so much debridement that I'm still using this crutch.

Wouldn't it be nice if God also did some debridement in our spiritual lives? Just go in and remove all that sinful, unhealthy stuff that accumulates and causes so many problems for us. He could eliminate anger and grief, guilt and depression, pride and prejudice. Bingo, it's gone!

Well, the amazing thing is that he does just that. That's the meaning of forgiveness. That's the result of confession and grace. That's the nature of his love. God is the spiritual surgeon who gets rid of all the sin that threatens to cripple us. But this spiritual surgery has to happen on a regular basis - day in and day out.

And like knee surgery, we need to go through a process of therapy to learn how to walk again. Sometimes we need a crutch or a cane or a walker to help us along. That therapeutic process, learning how to walk without the unhealthy tissue (sin), is what we call sanctification.

It's why we come to church, study the Bible, spend time in prayer. God is the ultimate therapist as well. The Holy Spirit works with us every day in spiritual therapy, teaching how to walk in new and holy ways.

May your walk with the Lord be upright, with no limps and no pain.

Limpingly yours,

Pastor Bob

SENIOR MOMENTS

Have you ever had a senior moment? You know what I mean, don't you? It's one of those times when you can't quite think of the right word to use, or maybe you misplace your glasses or your car keys, or you forget what day of the week it is. We all have them, some more than others.

A few weeks ago, I decided to make use of a gift card we had for Applebee's Restaurant. They offer Carside Service, which means you can just call in your order, tell them what kind of car you drive and what color it is, and when you get there they bring your food out to your car. After placing our order, I grabbed the gift card off my desk, drove to Applebee's, and when the waitress came out, I handed her the gift card. I wasn't exactly sure of the amount on the card, but suggested that she check it on her computer and let me know. She came back out quite quickly, handed me the card, and said: "This card is for Red Lobster." Oh...I grinned sheepishly as I reached into my wallet for cold, hard cash.

Another night, the very same week, Pat and I were on the east side of town and noticed the Marathon station there had gas for only $2.27 a gallon, some 18 cents cheaper than on the west side where we live. We pulled in, I filled up the tank, and went inside to pay.

When I came back out, Pat had turned on the key in order to read the odometer because we always keep track of mileage, gas purchases, etc. I got in, put the car in gear, stepped on the gas, and sat there, quite befuddled because the car didn't move.

The place was packed and the guy in the car behind me was waiting for me to pull out so he could leave too. I pressed harder on the accelerator, and still nothing happened. I was afraid the car was broken. It just wouldn't move, no matter how much gas I gave it. I had this worried look on my face as the driver behind me gave me an impatient glare.

Pat was wondering what I was doing. Finally she said: "The engine isn't running, silly!" (Or something like that.) Ah, no wonder the car wouldn't go. So I turned the key to start the engine and discovered that the car really WAS broken. It wouldn't start! I tried it several times, The guy in the SUV behind me was becoming more and more upset, making funny gestures with his hand and fingers. It was then that my dear wife bailed me out and informed me that I still had the car in gear and it won't start unless you have it in Park. Ohhh...another sheepish grin. Another senior moment.

Why am I telling you these things? Why am I making such lurid confessions? Well, first of all, to let you know that I am no different from the rest of you. We all have such times when we become a little confused, a little flustered, a little forgetful, a little befuddled. But secondly, to remind all of us that, as old as God is (infinitely old, remember?), he never has a senior moment. He never forgets your name. He never loses track of where you are. He never has to wonder how your body works or what you need to survive. He's always there for us, never missing an appointment, and never forgetting that we are sinners in need of forgiveness, grace, and love. Our God never fails us.

Mindfully or mindlessly yours,
Good Ol' What's My Name Again?

TAXES

Benjamin Franklin, in a letter to a friend in Europe, wrote: "In this world, nothing can be said to be certain but death and taxes." That may be true, but at least we don't have to die every year. Someone once described an optimist as a person who sets aside two hours to do his income tax returns.

Oh, I know there are software programs that you can buy – Turbo Tax and others. They walk you through the process, automatically asking you questions and then filling in the blanks on the appropriate tax form. For example, it says: Did you earn any interest on your bank accounts this past year? You type in the $1.67 you earned, and it fills out the proper form. When you're finished, the program will submit your returns electronically to the IRS. Then too, there are the organizations that will assist you with your taxes. AARP helps seniors at no cost, I think. To be really certain your taxes are correct, you can go to a professional – H & R Block for example – or to a CPA, a Certified Public Accountant. They will charge you several hundred dollars, but maybe it's worth it, not having to deal with the hassle of figuring out your own taxes.

I do my own taxes and hate it. That's because there are certain complications for ministers in the tax code. For one thing, I'm considered self-employed for Social Security purposes, which means my housing allowance is taxed at a higher rate than regular income. For another, nothing gets withheld from my paychecks during the course of the year, so I have to send in quarterly payments, based on my estimated tax burden. When it comes to doing my year-end taxes, it takes me several days of concerted effort. And lots of frustration. I am not a pleasant person to be around when it's tax time.

Every year there are changes to the tax code and new forms to fill out. The IRS used to send you a packet of materials with all the necessary forms and the instruction book for filling everything out. But now, in order to save money, the IRS doesn't send you anything. You have to go to the post office and the library to get some of the forms, and then you either need to make copies at the library or download the forms and instructions on your home computer. The United States is the only country in the world where it takes more brains to do your taxes than to earn the money to pay them.

One thing I find interesting about doing taxes is that they ask you how much you gave to charitable organizations during the year. Our deacons do a marvelous job of providing each of us with our giving statements, showing our offerings to Bethany during the previous year. This is critical when doing your taxes, but it's a joke among pastors that if the church really received what people reported to the IRS, our churches would be floating in money. Will Rogers said it this way: "The income tax has made more liars out of the American people than golf has."

Matthew, the tax collector in Jesus' little band of disciples, was hated by his countrymen, as was Zacchaeus, another tax collector. But Jesus told us to render unto Caesar the things that are Caesar's, so I'll pay my taxes. I just wish Caesar didn't have so much coming to him.

Taxingly yours,

Pastor Bob

MMM... GOOD

The other day I was talking to someone and she said she didn't really care for chocolate. Now I don't want to embarrass anyone, but her initials are Wilma Ver Hage. I was aghast! How can anyone not really like chocolate? I mean, that's like being against the American flag, against motherhood, and against church even!

Now I'm sure there are others out there who don't care much for chocolate, and I know there are some who aren't able to eat chocolate for medical reasons, but I think chocolate is our national food, more popular even than pizza or McDonald's.

Who doesn't love a Hershey Kiss? Who would turn down a Reese's Peanut Butter Cup? Who wouldn't go for a nice hot fudge sundae? Aren't there times when you just crave a piece of Dove chocolate?

How can the church survive without chocolate chip cookies?

Chocolate is one of God's greatest gifts to the human race. Giving someone chocolate is symbolic of love; it says you think the other person is sweet. Chocolate goes with many of our holidays – Christmas, Easter, Valentine's Day, Halloween. And I've read that chocolate even contains some chemicals that act in the brain to alleviate depression and raise a person's spirits. Dark chocolate has special ingredients that are supposed to slow down the aging process. It's practically a miracle food.

Actually, there is a miracle food, one that's even more potent and enjoyable than chocolate. Part of the wonder of this food is that it's 100% non-fattening. It contains no calories whatsoever, but it will strengthen you, eliminate depression, cure a variety of diseases, elevate your spirits, lower your blood pressure, and, in general, make you a better person all the way around.

In case you haven't guessed by now, it's the Bread of Life, the spiritual food God provides in his word. Now if we could only get people to crave the Bible the way we all (or almost all of us) crave chocolate.

Snickeringly yours,

Pastor Bob

IT'S ALL RELATIVE

What time is it? It's a simple enough question asked often enough, yet in this clock-studded society, the answer can vary surprisingly. Many people wear watches, but the younger generation keeps track of time on their cell phones. It seems strange that with a watch you can simply glance at your wrist to see what time it is, but if you have to look at your phone, you've got to dig it out of your pocket or purse. Some of us know exactly what time it is because we have a connection to the atomic clock in Fort Collins, Colorado that tracks time to 10 billionths of a second, or an accuracy of 1 second in a million years. It's based on the subatomic vibrations of a cesium atom. An old proverb says that a man with one watch knows what time it is, but a man with two watches is never sure. Just don't check Salvador Dali's watches.

Einstein tells us that time is relative, that the faster one goes, the slower time goes. If you reach the speed of light, time stops completely. Time is the 4th dimension, along with the other 3 spatial dimensions. The Bible says there's a time for every purpose under heaven (Ecclesiastes 3), but there never seems to be enough of it. Time, like the tide, waits for no one. We all have the same amount of time in a day, but we spend it differently.

So don't say you don't have enough time. You have exactly the same number of hours per day that were given to Helen Keller, Louis Pasteur, Michelangelo, Mother Teresa, and Leonardo da Vinci. The bad news is that time flies, but the good news is you're the pilot. But time is too slow for those who wait, too long for those who grieve, and too short for those who rejoice, but for those who love, time is eternity. The only reason for time, said one wag, is so that everything doesn't happen all at once.

Time heals all wounds, time is money, time is the partner of change. But we still don't know where all our time goes. We sleep away about one-third of it, and none of us knows how much time we have left, but the amount remaining diminishes steadily.

Jesus said, "My time is at hand," (Matthew 26:18), but he also reminded us that it's not for us to know the times and seasons which the Father has set (Acts 1). Paul tells us that we should "make the most of our time, because the days are evil." (Ephesians 5:16) The Psalmist says: "My times are in your hand," (Psalm 31:15) and "I will bless the Lord at all times." (Psalm 34:1) Peter reminds us that "with the Lord, one day is like a thousand years, and a thousand years are like one day." (1 Peter 3:8)

So what time is it? Time for me to wrap this up before I run out of time.

Timelessly yours,

Pastor Bob

ALLERGIES

Most of us have allergies. Some are allergic to tree pollen or to certain flowers or to cat dander or dogs or dust or mold or mildew or even certain perfumes. Pollen counts have been very high this spring, so many people are suffering more this year than in prior years. Some, who've never had allergies before, are having to deal with them this year. And I guess you can grow out of some allergies and grow into others. I've even heard that southwest Michigan is one of the worst places in the country for those with allergies. But at least there are medications, antihistamines, that will lessen the impact.

I'm allergic to cats, ragweed, and poison ivy. If I'm around a cat for very long, I'm in deep trouble. My eyes will itch and water for hours. How is it that cats know this? Whenever I go to a house where there's a cat, the first thing that happens is that the cat comes and starts rubbing against my leg and soon jumps onto my lap. Come August 15, when the ragweed begins to flower, I'll sneeze and blow my nose several hundred times a minute, and my eyes will water and my sinuses will drain and my throat will get sore and I'll cough a lot because of the drainage. And as for poison ivy, if the wind is blowing in the wrong direction, those itchy little blisters will break out all over my body, driving me crazy. I scratch those suckers in my sleep until they ooze and bleed and the poison gets into my blood stream and I end up going to the doctor to get a shot. I used to take baths in calamine lotion, but got tired of looking like the poster boy for Pepto-Bismol.

Allergic reactions are the way the body gets rid of the offending pollen. We sneeze or cough or our eyes water as a way of eliminating the irritant. That's a good thing, although it can be a nuisance. But poison ivy is another matter. Scratching the itch doesn't make the problem go away; it only worsens it. It's the oil in the plant that causes the problem, so scratching just spreads it around.

I know what poison ivy looks like, and I try to avoid it at all cost. But it seems I manage to get into it every year. It's like Paul saying that he knows the difference between right and wrong, and wants to do what is right and avoid doing what's wrong, but finds himself doing the wrong thing anyway.

Now if only we as Christians could develop an allergy to sin, and a means to avoid it and a way to expel it from our system when it becomes an irritant, we'd all be better off. But at least God provides the appropriate antihistamine to alleviate our guilt and eliminate the sin.

Sneezily yours,

Pastor Bob

DANCING

A couple of weeks ago, Pat and I were at a wedding reception. After the meal there was dancing. As at most receptions, there was the bride and groom dance, the mother of the bride dancing with the groom, the father of the bride dancing with the bride, and all the rest of the ritual dances. Then the dance floor was opened up for all the guests to dance. Pat and I had a chance to dance, which we don't get very often. It was nice. In fact, it was better than nice. We love to dance together, to hold each other close and sway to the music. We don't do the fast dances or the line dances or the chicken dance or the Macarena. But slow dancing is really nice.

It used to be that dancing was a forbidden activity for strict Christians. But now many churches even feature liturgical dance, with young women usually moving in a free-form manner to church music. Quite honestly, it takes some getting used to. Those of us accustomed to more traditional worship sometimes have a hard time with liturgical dance. But once you've witnessed it, it can be a very moving expression of worship and praise.

Dancing with the Stars is a current TV show that garners huge audiences. I've not seen it, but my parents love it. Several celebrities are paired with professional dancers and perform some of the traditional dances: waltz, fox trot, tango, etc. They compete to see who's the best. Dancing on TV has always drawn large viewership. The old Lawrence Welk show used to feature dancing. American Bandstand with Dick Clark was a hit when I was a kid. Teens did the jitterbug, the pony, the swim, the frug, the locomotive, the twist, and even the mashed potato and the Bristol Stomp.

Square dances used to be fun too, when you could do-si-do your partner and do a grand allemande left. And today's youthful generation has music videos and hip-hop, but I'm not sure that really qualifies as dancing.

In the Old Testament, Moses became angry when he came down Mt. Sinai with the Ten Commandments and saw the people dancing before the golden calf. But later, when the ark was returned to Jerusalem,

David danced in the streets in his underwear, much to the chagrin of Michal, Saul's daughter. And both Psalm 149 and 150 encourage God's people to dance as a form of praise. The writer of Ecclesiastes says there is a time to mourn and a time to dance.

I may not be the most nimble afoot, or the most graceful, but I can certainly appreciate it when other people move to the music. So if you want to dance in the aisles some Sunday morning, feel free.

Cha-cha-cha,

Pastor Bob

PILLOW TALK

What's the pillow like in your bed? Is it flat or puffy, hard or soft? Is it made out of foam or memory beads or goose down? I have two pillows. One is a typical foam pillow of medium height, but the other one, the one that actually goes under my head, is thicker and firmer, and also foam. The reason I have two pillows is because I tend to sleep on my side, and one pillow just isn't enough. When I'm on my side, if there's only one pillow, my head goes down too far and I wake up with a terrible crick in my neck. That extra pillow keeps my head at the right angle.

I've seen ads now for specialized pillows, depending on how you sleep. You can get a pillow for sleeping on your back or another one if you sleep on your side. They even sell one that has a hole in the middle for sleeping face down. You can buy a special pillow that just goes around your neck and cradles your head. Those are often used on airplanes or in the car. My mother uses a pillow that isn't much thicker than a sheet of paper. What's the point in that?

Then there are the pillow cases. I know that women often use a satin pillow case because then their hair slides around on it and doesn't get messed up as badly. There's nothing worse than waking up in the morning with bed-head. That's even worse than hat-hair.

Pillows are special objects for some people, almost like a doll or teddy bear or the security blanket that Linus uses in the Peanuts comic strip. I know our grandkids had favorite pillows that they used to carry around with them during the day. There's a certain comfort in a pillow.

Pillows can even be decorative. There are throw pillows that go on chairs and couches to bring out certain colors or to provide contrast. Decorators suggest using pillows to change the look of your rooms. I guess that's a cheap way to go – cheaper, at least, than buying all new furniture.

I think we take pillows for granted. Jesus once commented that "foxes have holes and birds have nests, but the Son of Man has nowhere to lay his head." And remember Jacob in the Old Testament? When he was on his way back to see his brother Esau, whom he had cheated out of the birthright, he stopped to spend the night at Bethel. In Genesis it says that "taking one of the stones there, he put it under his head and lay down to sleep." My study Bible says that in ancient times, this would not be uncommon, as some head-rests were even made out of metal. Ouch!

The important thing, I guess, is not what kind of pillow you have, or how many. What's really criti-cal is that, when you lay your head on your pillow at night, you can do so with a clear conscience, knowing that God has forgiven your sin and will grant you a good night of rest.

Sleepily yours,

Pastor Bob

ARRGH! MAKE
IT GO AWAY!

There it was – right in the middle of my face, right on the bridge of my nose. It looked ugly! I guess it served me right. I was horsing around with my grandsons on Thursday afternoon when it happened. One of the boys scratched me on the nose. It bled a little and I didn't think too much of it. But by Thursday night, it had scabbed over and looked bad.

Oh well, I thought, by Sunday it'll be gone and no one will be the wiser. But on Friday it looked worse, if possible. I put some antibiotic cream on it, hoping it would heal by Sunday. On Saturday, it was no better. More antibiotic cream. Still scabbed. Still ugly.

By Saturday night I was wondering if my wife had some makeup that would cover it up, make it less noticeable at least. But I thought, no, I'm just going to go to church with my nose looking the way it is. And there it was on Sunday morning for all the world to see. It really wasn't so bad. Maybe from a distance people didn't notice.

The nice thing is, nobody mentioned it. Maybe they just thought I scratched myself. But it felt terrible and I felt terrible – just like a teenager who gets a pimple on the day of the prom. There's really not much you can do about it.

Blemishes, pimples, scratches, and scabs are part of life. We all get them. And we're all embarrassed by them. It's just like sin. It affects all of us. It's part of life. It's part of our human nature. Ever since Adam and Eve, human beings have had pimples, scabs, and sin.

But the good thing is, God knows all about it. God knows we get pimples and scratches and scabs. God knows we sin. But he loves us anyway. And on top of it all, he makes provision for our scabs/sin. The human body has a way of healing itself. That's the way God made skin. But sin is another matter. We can't heal sin on our own. Our sin doesn't just go away in a day or three. It permeates our being and poisons our lives.

But wonder of wonders, God takes care of sin too. That's the whole reason Jesus came to this earth in the first place. Ever since that first sin, Jesus was preparing to come to earth and pay our penalty to bring healing for our sin. His death cured our sin once and for all. It's been washed away forever. And every time we sin, God is there to forgive us again.

Now we'll never have to be embarrassed to go to that eternal prom.

Clearasilly yours,

Pastor Bob

MY FAVORITE SEAT

I have a favorite chair at home. It's the one where I sit when I read, when I watch TV, when I do most anything. It's a rocker/recliner, so sometimes I even take a nap in it. I've probably spent so many hours in that chair that by now it must conform to that part of my anatomy that has the most contact with it.

Next to that chair are the books I'm currently reading, the magazines I read, the pen I use for crossword puzzles and Sudoku, my dictionary, a World Information Almanac, a one-volume ency-clopedia, a coaster for my Diet Coke, and numerous other artifacts of my daily existence.

When our kids visit, they seldom sit in that chair. They know it's "where Dad sits." They tell the grand-children "Don't sit in Papa's chair." It's not like I have a reserved sign on it. When we have company at our house, someone else usually sits there and I very rarely make them get up and go sit somewhere else.

I think most of us have a favorite chair, a place where we usually sit. It's true at home, and it's true at church. We have our favorite pew. It's where we usually sit on Sunday morning. Some folks even get here early to make sure they get THEIR seat.

A couple of years ago, if you remember, I had people change where they were sitting before we started worship. I was preaching that day about change, and I wanted people to experience this minor change. Those who sat in the balcony had to come down to the main floor. Those in the front had to move to the back or to the balcony. Those in the back had to come to the front. If you always sat on the north side of the center aisle, you had to go to the south side, and vice versa. Many of you said it was "weird" sitting someplace different, and the next Sunday, you were all back in your usual places. So much for change.

It's not all bad to have a "regular" seat in church. It helps me a lot. I can scan the congregation on Sunday morning and almost always know who's missing. "Their seat" is either unoccupied, or has someone else sitting in it.

One day, a man went to visit a church. He arrived early, parked his car, and got out. Another car pulled up near him, and the driver told him: "I always park in that spot. You took my place!" The visitor went inside for Sunday School, found an empty seat, and sat down. A young lady from the church approached him and stated: "That's my seat! You took my place!" The visitor was somewhat distressed by this rude welcome, but said nothing.

After Sunday School, the visitor went into the church sanctuary and sat down. Another member walked up to him and said: "That's where I always sit. You took my place!" The visitor was even more troubled by this treatment, but still said nothing.

Later, as the congregation was praying for Christ to dwell among them, the visitor stood, and his appearance began to change. Horrible scars became visible on his hands and his sandaled feet. Blood began to seep from his brow. Someone from the congregation noticed him and called out, "What happened to you?" And the visitor replied, "I took your place."

Seatedly yours,

Pastor Bob

ZZZZZ...

How well do you sleep? I know lots of folks, especially those of us who are beginning to age a tad, who have trouble sleeping at night. They get up several times to go to the bathroom, or to get a drink, or because they're dealing with pain. The writer of Ecclesiastes, in chapter 12, writes about what it's like to get older, and in verse 4, says that "men rise up at the sound of birds, but all their songs grow faint." In other words, even though our hearing may start to fade ("their songs grow faint"), the least little noise, such as a bird chirping, can wake us from a sound sleep.

Not so for me. I sleep the sleep of the dead. Once I'm asleep, a major earthquake or a tornado ripping the roof off the house might cause me to turn over, but not much ever disturbs my rest. Some people sleep like a baby – they wake up crying every 2 hours. I've noticed others who get their best sleep sitting in a pew on Sunday morning, listening to the preacher drone on.

On the nightstand next to my side of the bed, there's an alarm clock, a radio, and the telephone. Typically the alarm goes off about 5:45 a.m. When it does, I usually hit the snooze alarm for another 5 minutes or so of doze time, and also turn on the radio so I can hear the six-o'clock news before I actually get out of bed.

Sometimes, though, I'm in such a sound sleep that I get confused when the alarm goes off. I'll grab the telephone to see who's calling at that hour and wonder why all I get is a dial tone. The other day, the alarm was ringing and I didn't realize it was the clock. I kept trying to turn off that raucous noise by using the radio. I hit every switch and turned every knob, holding it up to my face in the dark, but nothing stopped that incessant ringing. "Why can't I shut this thing off?!" I said. Finally, Pat, amid gales of laughter, told me to put the radio down because it was the clock going off. Oh well.

Restful sleep is a wonderful gift from God. And our dreams can even be a way for the Holy Spirit to speak to our souls. But interrupted sleep is a burden many have to bear. Fortunately, as the Psalmist reminds us: "He who keeps you will not slumber. Behold, he who keeps Israel will neither slumber nor sleep." (Psalm 121:3-4) Our God never sleeps, ever. He's always there to listen to our prayers and our pleadings, even in the middle of the night.

Drowsily yours,

Pastor Bob

IT IS WRITTEN!

As many of you know, I write with a fountain pen. It's a Waterman that Pat gave me for Christmas several years ago. You may not count it as a "true" fountain pen because it uses cartridges. Some of you may remember actual inkwells in your desks at school, or buying small bottles of ink that you used in fountain pens with rubber bladders inside them. They were a mess. The cartridges are much neater.

I love the feel of my pen. It has substantial heft to it, and seems to fit in my fingers just right. I also like the way it writes. It's not a fine point, so there's a certain boldness to my handwriting. I use blue ink, although it doesn't copy well.

Some people prefer roller balls or felt tips. Many years ago I had a PaperMate that I was fond of as well. It had a smooth clicking action. Others just use cheap Bic pens, or their generic equivalent that you can buy 8 for a dollar. Maybe that's because they lose them or misplace them.

When I graduated from high school and college, I received Cross pens. They were considered very nice, and were typical gifts for graduates. When I left one of my previous jobs, I was presented with a gold Cross pen that was engraved with my name. It's still in my desk drawer.

At Bethany, we give visitors a pen with Bethany's name, address, and phone number on it. It's a pretty decent pen, actually. It writes smoothly and has that rubber grip where your fingers go.

As far as pens go, the top of the line, the Rolls Royce of all pens, is the Mont Blanc. They're made in France, I think, and cost upwards of several hundred dollars. I'm not sure they write 500 times better than a 19-cent Bic.

The only real pen that I'm concerned about is the one that God uses to write my name in the Book of Life. In fact, the pen doesn't really matter – it's what's written there than counts.

Inkily yours,

Pastor Bob

SERENDIPITY

Last week, when I pulled into the church parking lot early one morning, I noticed something where I park my car. On closer examination, it turned out to be two hunting knives with 6-inch blades, both in leather sheaths. One was fairly rusty, but the other was honed to a razor edge.

I wondered where they came from, who they belonged to, and what they were doing in the church parking lot.

Did they belong to kids who were just playing around and forgot them in the dark? Were they tossed there after being used in some nefarious activity? Did they indicate a potential increase in neighborhood crime?

I brought them into my office where they still sit. Should I call the police? That seems a little like over-kill. Should I ask around among the neighborhood kids to see if someone left them there and wants them back? That might be dangerous. I wasn't sure what to do, so I still have them.

Often we find things in unusual or unexpected places. That's called "serendipity." The dictionary defines "serendipity" as the faculty of making providential discoveries by accident.

Many times as we go through life, we encounter "providential discoveries." They represent the providence of God. He continually surprises us with grace and mercy. He often sends blessings our way that we don't deserve, and we aren't sure where they come from .

Sometimes, though, we fail to recognize his activity in our lives. Maybe we need to open our eyes in the semi-darkness to be more aware of all that God does for us.

I don't think God sent me two hunting knives. But I do believe that he provides for us daily.

Serendipitously yours,

Pastor Bob

GEMS IN THE SAND

You really need to look carefully for it. It's best to go early in the morning, before others have had a chance to look. Sometimes the sun hits it at just the right angle and it is easily spotted. Other times, you hunt and search and get confused by all the little shells that glisten in the light. And when you find some, it brings a sense of satisfaction, like finding treasure in the sand. I'm talking about beach glass.

Beach glass is a piece of regular glass that has been polished by the constant lapping of the waves and the back-and-forth motion in the sand. I assume it's there because someone threw a bottle into the lake and it broke into smaller pieces which then washed up on the shore. It comes in various colors, but usually it's a translucent white. Occasionally you find a green piece or a brown piece, and very rarely a blue or even pinkish piece.

Over the years that Pat and I have been going to Lake Michigan, we've found enough to fill a good-sized jar. Some of it is in a Mason jar that forms the base for a small lamp. We've even found some that were large enough that Pat's friend made her some jewelry – 3 necklaces, one each with green, blue, and white glass. Those pieces were probably about an inch-and-a-half long – giants, compared with the typically smaller pieces.

I like beach glass because it's a reminder of the joyous times we've had at the lake, of relaxing vacations, long walks, and long talks. I also appreciate it because it is transformed trash, something that was discarded (thoughtlessly) but was made beautiful by the actions of the lake.

I think we have beach glass in our lives. God takes the detritus, the trash, the stuff we don't even want to admit is there, and turns it into something beautiful and valuable. Our sins and shortcomings, our failures and hurts, can be transformed by God into hidden treasures. And when we discover those hard-earned gems, it's like an epiphany – God has indeed been at work in us again!

Searchingly yours, *Pastor Bob*

MOTHERS

May is the month for celebrating our mothers. Even if our moms are no longer living, we are still grateful for their impact on our lives. Some of us have been fortunate enough to have mothers and grandmothers and great-grandmothers who have touched our lives. Even aunts and neighbor ladies can be surrogate mothers. And this month we give thanks for those women in our lives who made us what we are today.

We remember growing up and the meals our moms made. No doctor can heal a skinned knee better than a mother's kiss. Knowing we made our mothers proud was success enough, no matter the endeavor. Our moms taught us to pray. Our mothers wrapped us in their arms when we needed that reassuring touch.

Mothers may not know much about baseball, but

they'll sit in the pouring rain and cheer their son or daughter whenever they're up to bat. Our popular music may drive them nuts, and our hair styles may make them grimace, but moms love us anyway. It's mothers who make sure our clothes are clean and pressed for school and church. It's a mother who nibbles the toes and tickles the tummies of little ones, just to see the smile on their faces and hear their hearty giggles.

It's a mother who watches with tears of joy as a son or daughter walks down the aisle to be married. It's a mom who tapes crayoned pictures to the refrigerator. It's a mother who stays awake, waiting expectantly for the sound of the door that indicates a teen-aged son or daughter has made it safely home from the prom. It's a mother who beams proudly as her child is handed that hard-earned diploma – whether it's from kindergarten, high school, or college. It's a mom who weeps silently when her child is hurt by malicious words or false gossip. It's a mother who stands in the doorway and utters a silent prayer as she wonders if that five-year-old is really ready to go off to school by herself. It's a mom who remains vigilant when her son goes off to war.

It's mothers who taught us much of what we know about God. We call God "Our Father," but he is sometimes more like a mother, or maybe we should say mothers are more like God. The nurture we receive from mothers resembles what we receive from God. The unconditional love of a mother teaches us about the love of God. The endless supply of forgiveness shows us how God deals with us as well. A prodigal son or daughter may come home to a loving father, but there's probably a loving mother standing right behind him, telling that father what to say and do.

To Israel, God says: "Can a mother forget the baby at her breast and have no compassion on the child she has borne? Though she may forget, I will not forget you." His love for us far surpasses the love of a mother for her child. Jesus said that he longed to gather the people of Jerusalem to him "as a mother hen gathers her chicks under her wings." This month we give thanks to God for all our mothers. We love you Mom!

A product of my mom (and my dad), I am childishly yours,

Pastor Bob

ABOUT THE AUTHOR

The Reverend Dr. Robert H. Terwilliger grew up in Wallkill, New York, a small village in the mid-Hudson Valley, some 70 miles north of New York City. He attended Rensselaer Polytechnic Institute and graduated from Hope College (B.A.), Western Theological Seminary (M. Div.), and International Seminary (Ph.D.)

Pastor Bob, as he is affectionately called, is ordained in the Reformed Church in America, the oldest Protestant denomination in the U.S. with a continuous ministry. He has served as the senior minister in Bethel Reformed in Harvey, Illinois, Hope Reformed in Kalamazoo, Michigan, and, for the last fifteen years, Bethany Reformed in Kalamazoo. He retired in 2013.

Bob also worked in the marketing department at the Kellogg Company in Battle Creek, Michigan, and as the marketing director for CRC Publications, the publishing ministry of the Christian Reformed Church in North America. From 1993 to 1998, he was a Mission Supervisor for the Reformed Church in America, overseeing mission work in Eastern Europe and Russia and among Native Americans in the U.S.

Since retiring, Bob and his wife, Patricia, have become involved at the Kalamazoo Civic Theatre, the third largest community theatre in the country. They have appeared in several plays and musicals, and Pat has volunteered in the costume shop. Pastor Bob also serves as a retiree chaplain for the denomination, caring for approximately 70 retired ministers, missionaries, and spouses in western Michigan.

Bob and Pat have a son and a daughter, and six grandchildren, all of whom live in Michigan. Another son, born with spina bifida, passed away in 2013. They live in Kalamazoo, Michigan.

CPSIA information can be obtained
at www.ICGtesting.com
Printed in the USA
LVHW021504140820
663173LV00018B/2545